EXTREME EMERGENCIES

Disclaimer

This sourcebook is for information and guidance purposes only. It is based on current (April 2004) research, knowledge, understanding and consultation with individuals and organizations with specific expertise in the fields of chemical, biological, radiological, nuclear and enhanced high-yield explosive (CBRNE) disasters. However, it is in no way intended as the provision of medical or other expert advice which is tailored or applicable to any particular circumstances, and in all cases the professional advice of a doctor and/or other medical professional or expert should be sought to deal with the specific medical or other circumstances of any particular case. The liability and responsibility for reliance on any information contained in this sourcebook rests with the person relying on it and not with the developer, editor, publisher or contributors of/to this sourcebook.

While the developer, editor, publisher and contributors have tried to ensure the accuracy of the information in this book, the fields of CBRNE are rapidly changing and except as stated below the developer, editor, publisher and contributors cannot be held responsible for the accuracy, completeness or usefulness of any information in this sourcebook or for any uses to which the information contained in this sourcebook may be put. The developer, editor, publisher and contributors exclude, to the fullest extent permitted by law, any and all liability which may be incurred as a result of any use or reliance by readers of or on any of the information contained in this sourcebook. Neither the developer, editor, publisher or contributors endorse any commercial product or service mentioned or advised in any part of this sourcebook.

We intend periodically to review and update this sourcebook to reflect changes in operational environments and threat assessments, new scientific advances and findings in microbiology and biotechnology, and technological research developments on CBRNE protective equipment and countermeasures.

EXTREME EMERGENCIES

Humanitarian Assistance to Civilian Populations following Chemical, Biological, Radiological, Nuclear and Explosive Incidents – A Sourcebook

ANTHEA SANYASI

Published by ITDG Publishing

The Schumacher Centre for Technology and Development, Bourton Hall, Bourton-on-Dunsmore, Rugby, Warwickshire, CV23 9QZ, UK

www.itdgpublishing.org.uk

© Merlin 2004

First published 2004

Reprinted in 2005

ISBN 1 85339 6028

A catalogue record for this book is available from the British Library.

ITDG Publishing is the publishing arm of the Intermediate Technology Development Group. Our mission is to build the skills and capacity of people in developing countries through the dissemination of information in all forms, enabling them to improve the quality of their lives and that of future generations.

Typeset by J&L Composition, Filey, North Yorkshire
Index by Indexing Specialists (UK) Ltd

Printed and bound in Great Britain by Antony Rowe Ltd., Chippenham, Wiltshire

Contents

Contents

Contents

Contents

Figures

Boxes

Tables

Preface

How can we prepare for a chemical, biological, radiological, nuclear or enhanced explosive (CBRNE) disaster? This was the question posed by the humanitarian charity Merlin in inter-agency discussions about the potential impact of a CBRNE event on the civilian population of a low-income country.

The consequences of even a small CBRNE incident could have massive dimensions, resulting in casualties, social disruption, evacuation and displacement. And a CBRNE disaster is something that NGOs working internationally may find themselves in the midst of without warning. In the more developed world, contingency plans presuppose high levels of emergency response capacity – with specialized equipment and technology and trained personnel. But disasters involving contamination, whether they happen by accident or intent, are equally likely in countries with fewer resources.

Planning for CBRNE disasters has been the preserve of expert governmental and international bodies, and of the military. Knowledge of the possibilities for humanitarian involvement has, until now, been poor. This sourcebook offers a first step towards bridging that gap. By opening up a very technical area, it offers a knowledge base on which NGOs can build in order to be ready to assist.

If a worst case incident should happen, humanitarian agencies could play a vital role in saving lives and reducing exceptional suffering. NGOs have a wealth of experience in providing shelter, food, medical care, water and sanitation following natural disasters and conventional wars. They could also be well equipped to deal with the psychosocial effects of such a traumatic event. Organizations with a health focus might contribute to the containment of infectious disease in the case of a biological emergency.

Drawing on guidelines from a wide range of sources, Merlin, collaborating with Médecins sans Frontières–Holland, Oxfam GB, Save the Children UK and the British Red Cross Society, has produced this sourcebook which outlines the functions and actions necessary in CBRNE incidents, so that humanitarian agencies can consider the issues in a well informed way.

Geoff Prescott, Chief Executive, Merlin

Acknowledgements

Merlin wishes to recognize contributions and support from a range of bodies and individuals:

International and intergovernmental organizations

Organization for the Prohibition of Chemical Weapons, The Hague; United Nations Environment Programme; Office for the Coordination of Humanitarian Assistance, Geneva and Brussels; World Health Organization – Health Action in Crisis, Geneva and Brussels; European Commission Civil Protection Unit, Brussels; International Committee for the Red Cross, Geneva; NATO: British, Belgian and French Army Medical Divisions; US Centers for Disease Control and Prevention; Humanitarian relief and development NGOs in the UK, Europe and USA.

UK Government national and regional services and departments

Department of Health, Health Protection Agency – Chemical Hazards and Poisons Division; British Metropolitan Police Service; British Transport Police; Fire Services Inspectorate; Home Office; London Ambulance Service; London Fire Brigade; London Resilience Team; London Underground; Ministry of Defence Army Medical School.

Individuals

With particular thanks to individuals in these organizations who provided information and guidance, and special thanks to Abdishakur Abdinur for temporary research assistance and Kaz de Jong, Médecins sans Frontières – Holland for contributing Chapter 5 on Psychosocial Support.

Funding sources

Merlin provided management support and a full-time office base, and the London School of Hygiene & Tropical Medicine, Public Health Unit, Conflict & Health Programme gave an honorary research fellowship to the writer, providing access to library and research facilities.

This sourcebook was jointly funded with grants from the Conflict & Humanitarian Affairs Department, Department for International Development (DFID), British Red Cross Society, Médecins sans Frontières–Holland, Oxfam GB and Save the Children UK.

Writer and editor

In preparing this sourcebook Anthea Sanyasi was a CBRNE Researcher for a consortium of international NGOs and an Honorary Research Fellow at the London School of Hygiene. She has a background in CBRNE health emergency planning for a British government strategic partnership team, and in disaster preparedness and response for the DFID Conflict & Humanitarian Affairs Department Operations Team. She has long-term experience in practitioner training and coordination of programmes within the refugee sector.

acknowledgements

Acronyms and abbreviations

ACAT	Assistance Coordination Assessment Team (OPCW)
APR	air-purifying respirator
ATSDR	US Agency for Toxic Substances and Disease Registry
BCPR	UNDP Bureau for Crisis Prevention and Recovery
BWC	Biological Weapons Convention
CBRNE	Chemical, Biological, Radiological, Nuclear and Enhanced high explosive sources
CDC	US Centers for Disease Control and Prevention
CIMIC	Civil Military Information Centre
CWC	Chemical Weapons Convention
DFID	Department for International Development (UK)
EADRCC	Euro-Atlantic Disaster Relief Coordination Centre
EAPC	Euro-Atlantic Partnership Council
EC	European Commission
ECURIE	European Community Urgent Radiological Information Exchange System
EMERCOM	Ministry of the Russian Federation for Civil Defence, Emergency Situations and Mitigation of the Consequences of Natural Disasters
EU	European Union
EWARN	Early Warning and Response Network (WHO)
FAO	UN Food and Agriculture Organization
GOARN	Global Outbreak and Response Network (WHO)
GPHIN	Global Public Health Intelligence Network (WHO)
HAZMAT	hazardous materials
IACRNA	Inter-Agency Committee on Response to Nuclear Accidents

IAEA	International Atomic Energy Agency
ILO	International Labour Organization
IOMC	Inter-Organization Programme for the Sound Management of Chemicals
IPCS	International Programme on Chemical Safety
MCDU	UN OCHA Military Civil Defence Unit
NATO	North Atlantic Treaty Organisation
NBC	nuclear, biological, and chemical (now termed CBRN)
NGO	non-governmental organization (humanitarian aid)
OCHA	UN Office for the Coordination of Humanitarian Affairs
OECD	Organisation for Economic Co-operation and Development
OPCW	Organisation for the Prohibition of Chemical Weapons
PAHO	Pan-American Health Organization
PPE	Personal protective equipment
REMPAN	Radiation Emergency Medical Preparedness and Response (WHO)
SCBA	self-contained breathing apparatus
SCF	Save the Children Fund
UN	United Nations
UNDAC	UN Disaster Assessment and Coordination
UNDMT	UN Disaster Management Team
UNDP	UN Development Programme
UNEP	UN Environment Programme
UNHCR	Office of the UN High Commissioner for Refugees
UNICEF	UN Children's Fund
UNIDO	UN Industrial Development Organization
UNITAR	UN Institute for Training and Research
UNJLC	UN OCHA Joint Logistics Coordination
UNSC	UN Security Council
UNSECOORD	UN Security Coordinator
WFP	World Food Programme
WHO	World Health Organization

Introduction

CBRNE – a new security risk

Chemical, biological, radiological, nuclear and enhanced high-yield explosive (CBRNE) hazards present new risks to international relief agencies and civilian populations. Although prohibitions on the use of chemical and biological weapons are now part of customary international law binding on all parties to armed conflicts, considerable concern remains about the increasing proliferation of arms and the effects that unregulated availability may have on civilian populations both during and after conflicts.

The current type of security threat can potentially be far more wide-reaching than conventional threats, affecting larger sections of civilian populations in 'mixed-conflict environments'. The aim of such violent conflict is to generate and inflict maximum impact through wide-scale terror, fear, injury, suffering and deaths, causing social and economic disruption and potential unrest. The increase in high-casualty, indiscriminate terrorist attacks on 'soft targets' anywhere in the world has become a disturbing trend.

There is also growing concern over the possible deliberate use of chemical and biological agents and the impact they might have on civilian populations. Periods of non-occurrence of biowarfare incidents may give the impression that few groups or rogue states have the competence or intent to use such means of terror, but there remains an unhealthy interest in some deadly pathogens and lethal chemicals and their means of refinement. Assuming an effective mode of dispersal and optimal meteorological conditions, scenarios using biological weapons, toxic chemicals and high-impact explosives can be devised, resulting in large numbers of casualties and deaths. An unsuspected virus may take longer to detect, but a local disease outbreak could rapidly become pandemic. Deliberate release of a hazardous chemical substance or an improvised radioactive explosive device in the form of a 'dirty bomb' could be catastrophic in the scale of physical devastation and fear, and could expose a field operation and its beneficiary population to the risk of highly lethal contamination.

Radioactive waste is found widely throughout the world, and poor security of such material is a concern. The dispersal of radioactive substances to contaminate air, food or water could render an area uninhabitable, and the mere threat of release of radioactive materials would cause widespread panic and anxiety. Explosion in a nuclear power plant would have similar effect to a radiological bomb. The indiscriminate use of simultaneous high-impact explosions and suicide bombings continues to inflict considerable injury and loss of life on civilian populations. Such events are unpredictable, and can occur in any operational area without warning.

Past and current CBRNE catastrophic incidents

Biological and chemical weapons have been used in the past primarily to terrorize an unprotected civilian population. As no-one can predict accurately when and where there may be exposure or contamination from a future incident – whether an intentional chemical or biological release or attack, or a transportation accident involving toxic chemicals or explosive material – contingency planning must be made on the basis of threat level and risk perception. Past incidents provide a shrill reminder of just some types of CBRNE threat and risk potential.

Chemical and biological warfare

In World War II, Japanese agents sprayed Chinese cities and villages with plague-infected fleas, which affected generations to come. More recently, in 2001 defoliants and unknown toxic gas were used by Colombian rebels. In 2002 a nerve agent threat was directed at Guam, and Iraqi security forces used napalm and other chemical weapons against the Iraqi population. Indiscriminate attacks included random carpet-bombing of rural areas with mustard gas and sarin against Iraqi Kurds in Halabja (Iraq) in 1988, and repression of the Marsh Arabs and other Shia communities following the 1991 Gulf War. Other biowarfare tactics have included deliberate contamination of water supplies and poisoning of fishing grounds. Highly toxic chemical warfare agents were released in civilian settings in Matsumoto (1994) and the Tokyo subway (1995) in Japan.

Industrial chemicals

Toxic weapons involving deliberate tactical use of industrial chemicals have been deployed by belligerent governments and non-state actors to affect outcomes of conflict. Such tactics have had military or large economic (soft) targets, but have had a severe impact on civilian populations. Notable events include deliberate release of industrial chemicals in World War I, causing 80 per cent of deaths. There are numerous examples of the use of toxic warfare during contemporary complex emergencies and violent conflict. Serbian forces launched attacks on toxic chemical plants, a pesticide production facility, national gas refinery and storage tanks in Croatia in 1993–95. Muslim forces threatened the use of chemicals in Tuzla in the mid-1990s. Pesticides and other chemicals in toxic weapons were used during the Israeli–Palestinian conflict. There were incidents of a poisoned water source in the Thai–Cambodian conflict in 1994; and use of unknown toxic chemicals in the Chechen–Russia conflict. Chlorine was one of the original war gases used in World War I (Ypres, France). Chlorine was also used in shells and for defence purposes during the Balkan conflict; rebels blew up a cistern with chlorine during fights in Grozny; a chlorine tanker was deployed as a weapon by a suicide bomber in Casablanca (Morocco); and a cyanide truck was hijacked in Mexico in 2002 with a view to deliberate release. Other types of planned industrial chemical incidents include oil pipeline bombings in Colombia in the 1990s, and a fuel oil–fertilizer bomb used in an attack on a federal building in Oklahoma City, USA. The growing incidence of chemical attacks is also seen in current protracted conflicts, for example bullets laced with chemicals in shoot-outs in Kashmir in the Pakistan–India conflict in 2003; suicide bombers coated with organophosphates in the Israeli–Palestinian conflict; and a planned chemical bomb and poison gas attack in Jordan in 2004.

Riot control

Chemical agents were used for riot control during World War I, and in Vietnam and Israel among other countries. In the Moscow theatre siege (2002) volatile substances were used to subdue terrorists and their prisoners, resulting in 129 deaths.

Accidental release of toxic gases

Accidental release of toxic gases in transportation accidents poses an additional hazard to civilians. Industrial and military accidents and crashes of tankers, trains and aircraft have caused major incidents. Catastrophic incidents of chemical and refinery explosions include a gas-well explosion release of highly toxic hydrogen sulphide in Gao Qiao, China (2003); industrial chemical site explosion in Toulouse, France (2001); and a chemical plant explosion in Taiwan. A massive explosion of a train transporting ammonium nitrate and oil caused large-scale deaths, injuries, destruction and lifeline disruption in Ryongchon, North Korea (2004). Also, derailment of a freight train carrying a lethal combination of toxic and flammable goods in Mississauga, northern Canada (1979) resulted in the largest evacuation in Canada's history. Other notable accidents include a gas explosion under trains in Ufa, Russia (1989); and derailment of a train carrying highly lethal toxic industrial chemical materials which caused a massive explosion, civilian deaths and destruction in Nayshabur, Iran (2003). Floods in Venezuela triggered large chemical spills and organic contamination in the coastal zone; and the most notable examples of toxic gassing of civilian populations are the catastrophic explosions of the nuclear reactor in Chernobyl, Russia (1986) and the chemical plant in Bhopal, India (1984).

Contaminated sites in conflict areas

These include unmarked chemical, biological and radiological facilities, and industrial waste sites. Post-war situations also pose the risk of unexploded ordnance from undetected cluster bomblets and sub-munitions. Nigeria's munitions dump explosion was a major incident; and a dumpsite in Somalia emitted highly toxic gases from materials causing a severe health hazard to the local population.

Bioterrorism

Bioterrorism involves deliberate threats or release of pathogens to create a climate of fear, and the tactical or systematic use of terror by individuals, groups, organizations or government bodies to coerce others and achieve their intent. The plotting ground for terrorist activity can be traced to both western and non-western countries where an unhealthy interest in all forms of poisons and chemicals has been under surveillance. Past and potential incidents include a series of fine-grade anthrax powder releases in postal attacks in the USA (2001); contamination of food at large gatherings (USA); interception of groups with ferrocyanide and maps of the Naples public transport system (Italy, 2003); and discovery of traces of ricin in the UK and USA.

Enhanced high-impact explosive incidents

A most likely type of terrorist weapon is an enhanced high-yield explosive device. Simultaneous high-impact bombings aim to induce large-scale death, destruction, disruption, chaos and fear among civilian populations. Attacks have been targeted at western and local communities in urban settings. Notable incidents include suicide bombings in Israel and the Occupied Palestinian Territories; Madrid, Spain; Moscow, Russia; Herat, Afghanistan; Istanbul, Turkey; Mumbai, India; Nasariya, Najaf, Baghdad and Basra, Iraq; Riyadh, Saudi Arabia; Karachi, Pakistan; Casablanca, Morocco; Bali and Jakarta, Indonesia; and in Tunisia; past attacks on embassies and high commissions in Jordan; Nairobi, Kenya and Dar Es Salaam, Tanzania; and, not least, the catastrophic events of 2001 in New York and Washington DC, USA involving the deliberate crashing of hijacked airliners into tower buildings.

Enhancing awareness of and preparedness for CBRNE incidents

An attack with a chemical agent would require a similar response to a major hazardous accident. Management of a large-scale disease outbreak, whether of natural or intentional origin, would need the same type of public health response. But major incidents of this nature may be beyond the coping capacity of local and regional emergency services, and would stretch the scarce resources of low-income countries that already face urgent public health crises with insufficient facilities. Inevitably, the impact of bioterrorism on developing nations would be much greater, owing to limited or absent health protection and specialized technology to counter such risks. International aid organizations operating in a resource-poor country can try to gauge the potential capacity for a host nation to respond and consider how public health preparedness can be enhanced.

In the past, severe health hazards and risks posed by biowarfare events have impeded involvement of non-specialist agencies. With the increasing threat, a degree of preparedness by humanitarian aid agencies becomes essential when operating in a CBRNE-risk environment, or suddenly finding oneself in the midst of a major incident of this kind. Some element of danger is inherent in most humanitarian work in crisis and violent conflict situations, but a deliberate or inadvertent release of chemical or biological agents or radiation exposure poses additional risk to field staff and beneficiaries. The NGOs inevitably will have to assess the balance of risk of such events against other security, health and safety risks.

As the current conflict environment is unpredictable, an NGO's security and risk-management strategy should include provision for appropriate preparation and personal protection in their pre-deployment contingency planning. Existing risk assessments and response strategies can be adapted to include CBRNE hazards as specialized threats in high-risk areas. Overall, the best way to mitigate any event would be to adopt an 'all-hazards risk approach' for planning and preparedness, and produce relatively simple but sustainable policies and procedures adequate for all humanitarian emergencies.

For disaster relief organizations, principles of risk management for response to chemical or biological incidents will overlap with operating procedures for natural and other man-made disasters and emergencies. Mitigation measures will often be similar, and lessons learned and best practices can be applicable to both human-made and natural disasters. A community's capability for managing such incidents is an essential component of preparedness. However, the most prominent consequence of incidents involving biological and chemical agents is their ability to cause mass casualties, overwhelming local medical resources and facilities. Where public health infrastructure is resource-poor and specialist training and equipment are lacking, multilateral and international organizations can try to build local emergency response capacities rather than creating new ones. But in a sudden incident where the coping capacity is severely overstretched, NGOs' rapid humanitarian response capability in situ may be vital to relieving severe human suffering.

Procedures drawn from natural disaster management may prove useful, and specific knowledge of CBRNE hazards, their characteristics and immediate effects could help guide the course of action for NGO personnel to assist the affected population with humanitarian relief. Potential effects of exposure will present challenges for NGO staff who are not equipped or trained in the use of personal protective equipment. Emergency operations in the 'hot exclusion zone' and decontamination in the 'warm zone' would have to be restricted to specially equipped and trained frontline rescuers, but after initial rescue efforts the essential priority of humanitarian aid organizations would be to sustain the lives of survivors in the 'clear zone'.

Potential role of humanitarian aid organizations

In situations of disruption and displacement, where the affected population has been evacuated or has fled the danger area, general emergency-planning measures and response procedures familiar to a humanitarian relief NGO would form the basis of humanitarian action in a technical emergency. Individual NGOs already possess the skills, knowledge and experience relevant to aspects of post-incident support.

An NGO's operational know-how, based on a particular technical capacity in emergency relief such as shelter, relief logistics, water and sanitation, health protection and primary healthcare, could be geared towards a technical emergency that might require assistance with secondary decontamination of victims and emergency treatment of casualties. Similarly, an NGO's rapid response capability for provision of humanitarian assistance might be drawn on to mobilize emergency shelter and medical aid and supplies. Care and assistance to displaced people might also require additional food aid, household and cooking equipment, clothing, water and sanitation, among other basic relief.

Humanitarian organizations involved in healthcare in crisis situations may have valuable experience in biological interventions and management of contagious disease epidemics, which could be redirected towards treatment of an 'unusual' disease outbreak. It seems feasible, too, that NGOs with experience in medical relief may be able to assist in a public health response and secondary triage and treatment of victims outside the danger zone, given that a hospital-based specialist response may be limited in some situations.

Technical capacity building and preparedness for handling some of the health effects of CBRNE hazards could enhance existing capabilities. New knowledge and skills may be needed for decontamination and biocontainment procedures, and for use and delivery of specialized treatment. To this end training modules, manuals, guidelines and treatment protocols can serve as tools to acquire specific knowledge and guidance in this specialized field.

Introduction to the sourcebook

This CBRNE sourcebook is for international NGOs providing humanitarian assistance in middle- and low-income countries. As civilian populations in potential CBRNE at-risk environments are of particular concern, the sourcebook provides a generic guide for mitigation and humanitarian response to affected populations outside the immediate danger zone. It seeks to enhance knowledge of CBRNE risks and their acute effects to safeguard the health and safety of NGO field staff and assist planning for the most appropriate humanitarian response actions in an incident.

An NGO's policy on involvement in life-threatening situations will be influenced by its mandate, technical competence and priority objectives. Part I, on Managing the Crisis, covers five chapters. Chapter 1, on *Strategic management* outlines key points for policy and decision-making for senior management at head office and field levels concerning staff deployment and protection and potential humanitarian responses in a post-CBRNE context.

A proactive approach to an 'all-hazards' risk-management strategy will involve preparedness and mitigation measures. As components of emergency preparedness, good public health, near real-time surveillance and alert systems will be essential in monitoring emerging infectious diseases. Chapter 2, on *Tactical management*, provides a guide for early warning and preparedness through mechanisms for systematic vigilance, observation, surveillance and information gathering. Drawing on a risk-analysis approach it raises awareness of the necessity for vulnerability reduction measures and risk assessment of potential CBRNE hazards in the area, region or country in which NGOs are operating.

Non-governmental organizations already play a vital role as first responders in complex emergencies and natural disasters. Given the emergency or disaster relief mandate of many, it is reasonable to assume that an aid organization would wish to respond to the immediate humanitarian needs of affected beneficiaries in countries of operations. In a technical emergency a readiness and humanitarian response strategy could support the local medical response and public health system in their management of victims during the early phases. Chapter 3, on *Field staff safety*, provides checklists and a step-by-step guide for personal protection measures and rapid action within critical timelines of a sudden event. Chapter 4, on *Operational management*, focuses on safe site planning and humanitarian assistance to affected civilian populations in the post-contamination stage of an incident.

Chemical agent or radiation exposure could have a particular impact on the physical and mental health of a victim in the short and long term. Chapter 5 provides guidance on culturally appropriate psychosocial support which may be required following an incident of this kind.

Chapter 6 gives a snapshot overview of the range of CBRNE hazards, their characteristics, clinical effects and required treatment.

Chapters 7–10, respectively, raise awareness of key indicators, characteristics, effects and appropriate response measures to a release of chemical and biological agents, radiological or nuclear exposure, and high-yield explosive incidents. To an extent, the aftermath of such emergencies can be foreseen by the systematic application of scenario methods and lessons learned from past events. Although preparation must be generic and cannot be based on a single set of scenarios, brief scenarios and case studies are presented on the different types of risk and hazards to guide humanitarian response planning, describing immediate impact and health effects, and essential emergency response actions that must initially be made by the respective first responders.

Part III of the sourcebook contains ten sections on resources. Resource I lists some of the constraints and limitations of using detection and monitoring devices, in recognition that trained specialists are required for effective detection, identification and diagnosis of biological, chemical and radiation incidents.

Management to limit health risks to staff involves a range of checks and balances, not least consideration of the need for personal protective measures and kits. Resource II highlights essential points about personal protective equipment (PPE), the different levels of PPE required for frontline emergency responders, and the need for special training. It provides checklists for basic 'survival and response kits', which NGOs could carry in their rucksacks or vehicle should field staff find themselves in the vicinity of a chemical, biological or radiation incident.

Resource III, *Medical countermeasures*, explains briefly the limitations of pre-exposure vaccines against biological agents, and why stockpiling of medicines for post-exposure treatment is not recommended by the key international public health organizations.

Resource IV focuses on *Medical protocols for key chemical agents*, describing the type, characteristics clinical effects, and required treatment and management of chemical casualties of key chemical agents likely to be used in a deliberate release.

Resource V describes decontamination procedures for victims of chemical contamination where emergency response facilities for technical emergencies are limited in resource-scarce, low-income countries.

Resource VI, *Medical protocols for key biological agents*, outlines their effects and provides basic guidance on appropriate response measures and treatment of 'unusual or emerging infectious diseases' by medical professionals. Unsuspected disease outbreaks may have a short lifespan, while others could be highly contagious for some time. Where primary and secondary healthcare facilities are resource-poor or non-existent, temporary emergency structures for triage, quarantine, isolation and medical treatment may need to be mobilized.

Resource VII outlines provisions for special protection measures and treatment of radiation and nuclear exposure from civil nuclear site incidents.

Lack of specialized technical resources and knowledge and limited experience can be constraining factors to NGO involvement in a post-chemical or biological incident. Understanding CBRNE threats and hazards, how these can impact on NGO operations and civilian populations, and the best way to respond will help mitigate their consequences. As a tool for humanitarian organizations to improve their knowledge and skills on CBRNE incidents and their effects, Resource VIII provides a suggested curriculum for training and capacity building of NGO and local capability, and provides a list of training establishments that might offer courses or educational materials on CBRNE awareness.

Resource IX contains a directory of CBRNE-related organizations and conventions which can be accessed for reliable and credible information and professional guidance.

Resource X provides pocket-sized quick reference cards to serve as practical checklists for indicators and response actions for CBRNE incidents.

PART I
MANAGING THE CRISIS

CHAPTER 1
Strategic management

Senior managers and emergency operations planners at strategic level in non-governmental organizations (NGOs) will have a range of factors to consider in the development of policy and good practice in the event of chemical, biological, radiological, nuclear and enhanced high-yield explosive (CBRNE) incidents. An NGO's policy on involvement in life-threatening situations will be influenced by the individual NGO's mandate, humanitarian objectives, technical competence and priority objectives.

NGO objectives

Humanitarian objectives of NGOs seek to promote the fundamental humanitarian principles of humanity, neutrality, impartiality and independence enshrined in International Humanitarian Law. These aim to reinforce the core of humanitarianism, which is to:

- save, preserve and protect lives

- respect human life and the 'right' to life and dignity

- alleviate extreme suffering

- mitigate and minimize the impact of a hazard or incident

- provide assistance solely on the basis of need.

NGOs seek clear boundaries between humanitarian relief work and foreign policy security strategy, and in any response action would want to safeguard respect for humanitarian principles.

Strategic objectives would be to provide an independent, neutral, humanitarian capacity to respond to civilian populations who are affected by a man-made or natural disaster anywhere in the world.

Specific objectives in a deliberate or accidental CBRNE incident may be to:

- contribute to effective early warning

- maintain the health and safety of staff responding to a CBRNE incident

- coordinate with on-scene emergency response organizations

- assist fleeing populations with decontamination guidance
- assist casualties and victims in the safe 'clear' zone with medical aid and humanitarian relief.

Key considerations

Chemical, biological, radiological, nuclear and enhanced high-yield explosive hazards pose tremendous challenges and increased risks to emergency response organizations. As traditional responders to global humanitarian crises, NGOs will need to make informed organizational decisions on the insecure risk environment following a chemical, biological or explosive incident, and on whether to suspend operations, evacuate from the area or seek safety in a safe building. If the affected population requires humanitarian assistance outside the contaminated zone, key considerations would have to be made on the basis of a range of questions (Box 1.1).

Box 1.1   Checklist for involvement

Type and magnitude of the emergency?

Context situation of the emergency (e.g. armed conflict)?

Location of the incident and logistical accessibility?

Affected population, size and dispersal range?

Physical and material needs?

Necessity for outside intervention?

Coping capacity and ability of national public health and emergency services?

Need for support to local structures?

Who can or will respond, and under what circumstances?

What collaborative arrangements with other organizations could be developed?

What is the NGO's own capacity in terms of appropriate resources and skills capability?

Which staff would be utilized and in what circumstances?

Could involvement affect the safety of NGO staff?

Have CBRNE guidelines been incorporated into the NGO's security planning and threat assessments?

What specialist PPE might be required, and how would it be accessed?

Have staff been trained or equipped for use and maintenance of PPE and decontamination of people?

Key policy issues at headquarters and in the field

It will be important to have a policy statement based on an individual NGO's involvement or intervention in the post-exposure stage of an incident. A CBRNE policy and operational parameters would need to be aligned with the NGO's organizational mandate and technical specialist area. Formulation of such a policy is likely be influenced by the NGO's:

- vision, mandate, technical competence and priority objectives

- policy on involvement in life-threatening situations (types, degree of risk)

- level of acceptable risk (informed consent procedures by staff deploying to at-risk areas)

- risk assessment – ability to deliver assistance weighed against the risks

- political considerations and sensitivities

- type and level of response (based on capacity and capability)

- evacuation policy and plan

- commitment to NGO's charter and Code of Conduct for the International Red Cross and NGOs

- informed debate – NGO/military relations, proximity to military forces and policy on channels of communication with military planners/actors (maintaining clear and separate mandates of operations which permit only NGO humanitarian relief operations).

Strategic considerations in a technical emergency will involve an NGO's decision-making process on its involvement, consequence management, project and programme continuity, effective communication and media handling, and dealing with the health and safety of staff.

Personnel issues – protection of frontline staff

Further considerations may include human resources issues and procedures for deployment of field staff, including the following.

- Preservation of staff health, safety and well-being.

- Employer's responsibility for personal safety (duty of care) which requires adherence to health and safety regulations. Legislation regarding an employer's duty of care responsibility for employees' health and safety will be drawn from national health and safety legislation, and there is a question as to whether it would be legally applicable outside the country of the NGO's headquarters. Health and safety in-country would be assessed on the basis of a country or area threat and risk assessment, and NGOs must have policies and procedures for this. According to the UK Health and Safety Executive there are no 'safe limits' for chemical and biological warfare. Limits are stipulated only for toxic chemical infrastructure breakdown in peacetime conditions, for which protocols are set.

- Safe workplace – assessed security environment, appropriate equipment and resources, access/withdrawal policy, information and training.
- Safe systems – incident planning, training and procedures such as briefings and communication.
- Provision of effective communication between field staff, country office base and head office.
- Staff briefing on potential hazards of CBRNE high-risk environments.
- Staff informed consent for risk and involvement in CBRNE incidents (this is a signed document to ensure NGO staff members understand the risks).
- Contract waivers – staff members freely and voluntary undertaking their assignment with all associated risks.
- Health check – at pre- and post-assignment stages.
- Pre- and post-vaccination of frontline humanitarian workers, if appropriate.
- Procurement and use of PPE kits.
- Dress code – advice on appropriate field clothing.
- Emergency medical kits.
- Medivac procedures – arrangements for the medical evacuation of a sick or wounded individual.
- Field operation evacuation plan, procedures and drill.
- Stress management workplace practice and training.
- Insurance liability and cover – some insurance companies will insure exposure risk, but some may offer limited cover where there is a perceived threat. There may be exclusion clauses and limitations concerning CBRNE risk environments (e.g. benefits may not be payable for death or injury resulting from war, military activities, exposure to exceptional danger, effects of terrorism or radiation incidents). Ultimately employers will have liability for cover in countries not covered by insurance companies. It will be necessary to have proper risk-management strategies in place and to provide evidence of managing risks properly, including provision of a security plan, training, guidelines, briefing and debriefing.
- Standard operating procedures.
- Personal protection and effectiveness training and measures.
- Training on CBRNE issues – identify focal points and competencies.

Disaster management strategy

A disaster management strategy should examine disaster management capabilities for early warning, alert, prevention and preparedness; and develop a policy for ensuring appropriate procedures, equipment, resources and training for frontline staff who may be at risk from these additional hazards.

An emergency preparedness policy is needed for working in a suspected at-risk CBRNE environment: NGOs may wish to include policy statements and security and safety guidance, drawing on the examples in Box 1.2.

Box 1.2   Policy statements

Health and safety

- No member of staff would be permitted to remain or work in an area of known or suspected CBRNE contamination where safety cannot be reasonably assured.

- No-one will be compelled or coerced into remaining in or re-entering a suspected or confirmed technical disaster area against their will, or be allowed to do so without their informed consent.

- If unable immediately to leave a contaminated area (such as during quarantine), the priority will be the preservation of staff safety and well-being.

- The NGO will ensure all staff members are fully informed of potential technical emergencies in their work area.

Movement restrictions

Staff may be asked to comply with the following procedures:

- no travel or movement outside of the project locality – daytime and night-time

- authorization must be given for all movements and routes

- frequency and locations of contacts for communication must be provided

- latest departure and arrival times and evacuation routes must be stated.

Radio and communications

- Standby times: day/night/week/weekends.

- Calling frequency, radio checks, VHF communication: where and when mandatory.

CHAPTER 2

Tactical management

Tactical management will be an area of consideration for head office and field programme managers at regional and country levels. It incorporates a risk-management strategy that includes vulnerability reduction and mitigation of potential CBRNE hazards among other security risks in middle- and low-income countries.

Field operation vulnerabilities

Programme operations of NGOs in facility-poor environments can be at risk to overt threats, deliberate acts of chemical or radiation exposure, or covert risks of a less detectable biological agent. As a risk-reduction and preparedness measure, NGOs might consider factors that increase the vulnerability of field projects and the beneficiary community to such threats.

Hazard vulnerability analysis and risk-reduction measures

Analyses of CBRNE hazards and vulnerability will include identification of high-visibility or symbolic targets with the potential for creating public fear or attack on vital systems, structures and critical lifelines, such as power and water supplies. Where possible, discrete liaison with appropriate civil government bodies or civil/military personnel can guide awareness of high-risk security areas which should be avoided. NGOs should try to gauge the vulnerability of the location of a field project site and its proximity to industrial chemical sites or nuclear power plants and routes of passage for hazardous material. Events involving VIPs, political and religious events pose potential security risks, and airfields, ports, United Nations posts and government offices can also be hard targets for terrorist threats. A common measure to reduce vulnerability and health risks of chemical hazards would be to locate humanitarian programmes at a distance of at least 5–10 km from industrial chemical sites, military structures and government installations.

If the project site has high visibility, consider the value of NGO site assets or relief goods and the external image of staff and programmes. To maximize safety and security measures, assess the effectiveness of:

- field security strategy and plan
- protection of vulnerable infrastructure
- site and vehicle management
- location of fire-fighting equipment
- contingency plans for evacuations
- medivac procedures
- level of training and equipment of local civil emergency response organizations
- capacity and capability of local health facilities.

Other factors that affect vulnerability and resilience include access, availability and quality of shelter and personal protective survival equipment; and training in decontamination procedures of potential NGO emergency and medical responders.

Site vulnerability reduction measures

Non-governmental organizations could compile a vulnerability list and conduct an assessment of their field operations. Security and vulnerability reduction measures might include:

- buildings security – heavy barriers or staggered cement flower pots around the building
- windows – shutters, bars or mesh screens to protect window entry
- security guards – visible security presence with patrols
- intruder detection – alert and surveillance systems and measures
- controlled-access entry procedures – reception desk, registration or some form of sign-in and sign-out system
- visitors' parking – restriction to 300 feet (approximately 90 metres) from the building
- goods delivery – separate entrance with identification controls
- restricted areas – security controls for intrusion detection
- emergency exits – fire escapes, fire doors and fire extinguisher equipment and sprinkler system, regular fire alerts, evacuation drills, routes and relocation sites
- air-handling system – to control ventilation and air-conditioning systems
- backup power sources – additional generators
- security communications – adequate handheld and satellite radio systems
- first-aid kits – in office, in vehicles and at project sites
- potable water facilities – in case of polluted or contaminated main water supply

- emergency storage capabilities – secure site for sensitive material and equipment

- incident reporting – of unusual events, suspicious activity or strange occurrences.

Threat assessment and risk-strategy policy

Awareness of CBRNE risks should be based on security measures for conventional warfare, mixed threats, and risk of non-conventional weapons. Early warning systems and contingency planning are essential mechanisms for disaster preparedness and mitigation. Adopting a risk-analysis approach, an NGO's security policy and contingency measures should be extended, with an annex to include assessment of risk potential to chemical, biological and radiation exposure.

Risk perception is as important as risk assessment. Given that it is difficult to predict an incident involving exposure to a contaminant, an NGO's regional or country office may wish to make every reasonable effort to gauge the probability of certain types of scenario, to identify known threats and vulnerabilities relating to past technical emergencies, and to implement measures to ensure staff safety against all types of hazard.

Staff health, safety and security

Safety of staff in a CBRNE-related incident should take precedence over other concerns to avoid staff becoming casualties themselves. This might involve identification of all pertinent preparation and response agencies, followed by an appropriate level of coordination to ensure the highest level of safety. The following measures may assist in the process.

- Country offices conduct a thorough safety and security assessment to determine threats and vulnerabilities for a potential technical emergency – deliberate or accidental.

- Appoint security focal points and integrate chemical, biological and radiological hazards, as 'specialized threats', in security plans and management.

- In the field constant companion contact list, containing details of important contacts in the field and at head office, including numbers for rapid notification of the emergency services in the event of an incident.

- Mainstream regular surveillance and standardized reporting of incidents by staff.

Risk assessment of the exterior environment – basic principles

- Establish the context and identify, analyse and evaluate threats and risks.

- Contain known risks and improve preparedness.

- Apply disaster-management principles to understand the type and magnitude of the risk, causes and comparable risk.

- Put the possibility of deliberate attacks into a broader risk-management perspective.

- Place emphasis on risk awareness of the range of event types possible, and adopt an integrated 'all-hazards' approach to mitigate events and develop strategies to minimize their destructive effects.

Given that all scenarios are hypothetical and unpredictable, it is impossible to establish a clear CBRNE risk assessment. The list below is not exhaustive, but expands on some of the variables within scenarios that may have an impact on the probability of CBRNE deliberate release.

Situational awareness of risk environment

- Threat indicators may differ by country, rural or urban setting, and culture. Be vigilant and continuously examine security situations for changes that might increase the likelihood of a threat.

- Determine threat levels by assessing the existence of subversive elements in the region or area, the capability to deliver attacks, the intent of past threats and actions, past events history and threats of terrorist activity against specific targets.

- Indicators of an at-risk environment include regional and political instability, existence of open conflict, belligerent relations and dynamics between warring parties, the spread and strategic importance of the conflict, and the likelihood of use of weapons. The intensity of conflict is also an important factor in assessing the potential for use of a destructive explosive device. Intelligence reports will be extremely useful at this point, and a sound security network is essential. Security information sources might include government departments, embassies, ministries of internal or foreign affairs, United Nations security officers, NGOs, civil military information centre (CIMIC) officers (for military information), and local knowledge.

- Actor mapping includes assessing the political position of actors who play an active role in a conflict, which might help gauge the seriousness of commitment to using specific chemical or biological weapons or agents. Be aware of the past history and stated policies of state and non-state actors, and their relationships.

- Be observant of locations of military bases and security forces, strategic and iconic buildings, and possible soft targets such as international financial centres, public transport stations and large-scale events and gathering places.

- Consider the level of probability that team members and the local population might become exposed to a chemical substance release or spillage, an unusual disease or a nuclear accident. Envisage potential methods of delivery, transmission and extent of an attack, including range of weaponry and possibility of air release (e.g. short-range, hand-held or vehicle-carried missiles or shells, or a suicide bombing). In the event of exposure, imagine the extent of a release and how the geography of the area might affect it.

Chemical plants and nuclear reactors

Non-governmental organizations can assess whether an operation is in a potentially at-risk area by drawing on local knowledge of what chemical and nuclear plant capability the region possesses. They can also map the locations of hazardous industrial chemical plants and nuclear installations near populated areas. Knowing the 'danger signs' of hazardous materials sites and the perimeters of the information zones and safety zones around an industrial chemical plant would also be useful. Inquire whether the local population resident in the information zone (2–3 km radius of a site) has been given:

- information on the basic site activity
- a description of the type of hazardous substances stored
- a description of the emergency warning signal, e.g. activation of a siren
- information on emergency action, e.g. effective sheltering advice, tuning in to radio frequencies for further instructions and refraining from using telephone landlines.

Also, observe HazMat signs (yellow triangle containing a symbol on drum of chemical substance) which indicate immediate emergency action required by hazardous materials specialists (including level of PPE and evacuation procedures); see Chapter 7, *Key chemical agents*.

Civil/military information centres (CIMICs)

Depending on the location, size, scope, method of delivery and type of weapon or agent used, situations involving chemical, biological and/or nuclear weapons may necessitate the use of NATO military specialists and equipment. It could be useful to establish reliable access points to civil/military information structures at field level and at headquarters. This may be through civil/military liaison officers and civil affairs units. It might also be tactical to establish what the extent of a military intervention would be in search and rescue, detection and decontamination in a chemical, biological or radiation incident. While humanitarian principles of independence and neutrality will be paramount for an NGO, the safety of staff and beneficiary populations may take precedence over concerns of avoiding military contact.

Security forces preparations

Movements of NGO teams in an area under CBRNE threat will often be determined by military movements in the area. It is unlikely that military intelligence would be directly transmitted to civilian organizations, although there may be some observations from military preparations. Military alerting networks provide information, enabling commanders to call for different alert levels. Each of these alert levels demands putting on items of protective gear. Military mission-oriented protective posture and regimes (NATO 1996) are important indicators of gearing up for a heightened threat or risk. NGOs should be aware of the designation of restricted areas, military convoys, guarded areas and new checkpoints.

NATO graduated levels of nuclear, biological or chemical (NBC) threat and NBC dress states

1 **Zero** – the belligerents have no known offensive NBC capability (respirator carried within unit supply chain)

2 **Low** – the belligerents have an offensive NBC capability but there is no indication of its use in the immediate future (respirator carried, protective equipment available)

3 **Medium** – NBC weapons have been used in another area or operations and/or there are strong indications that the belligerents will use these weapons in the immediate future (respirator, boots and gloves carried, suit worn, hood down)

4 **High** – NBC attack is imminent (respirator and gloves carried, suit hood down, boots worn).

5 **State Black** – NBC attack has been detected (NBC physical protection is worn, respiratory equipment carried, suit hood up, boots and gloves worn).

Information circulating among the local populace may also be an indicator of an impending threat.

Horizon scanning, surveillance and advisory mechanisms

Horizon scanning is a system that can be used to combat emerging infectious diseases and wider public health protection threats with strong surveillance, early recognition, rapid expert response and effective links with other national and international bodies. Surveillance can provide an important public health advisory alert, and routine sensitive and near real-time disease surveillance systems are essential in disease outbreaks, particularly those caused by biological agents. Information from a variety of sources can be accessed to detect epidemiological indications of a possible event via national public health mapping and international epidemiological surveillance mechanisms. An NGO may also join an alert network for preplanned heightened information systems for outbreaks of illness. Such networks include:

■ World Health Organization (WHO), which has responsibility for supporting epidemiological surveillance and disease outbreak responses

- Global Outbreak Alert and Response Network (GOARN), a technical collaboration of existing institutions and networks which pool human and technical resources for the rapid identification, confirmation of and response to, outbreaks of international importance; several epidemic diseases within the scope of the WHO surveillance and response programme have been associated with biological warfare

- Global Public Health Intelligence Network (GPHIN), a semi-automated electronic system to identify warning information about epidemic threats and rumours of unusual disease events.

See Resource IX, *Directory of organizations and conventions*, for more information and other international surveillance mechanisms and agencies.

Risk-management tools

Once the risk assessment is complete, the appropriate mitigation, preparation and response procedures could be incorporated into an NGO's regional or country office contingency plan.

An NGO's emergency response plan is an important component of tactical management. All field personnel could benefit from learning and routinely reviewing the plan and procedures as a tool to recognize risks, and enhance understanding and effectiveness.

Medivac procedures would provide information on facilities, hospitals, health clinics, laboratories, specialist facilities, burns and trauma units, ambulance service, doctors in country or outside, and transportation.

An emergency evacuation plan requires effective VHF communication procedures between field staff and headquarters on radio checks, calling frequency, locations of contact and evacuation routes.

Immediate evacuation may be required in the event of an industrial chemical or radiation release. Be aware of rules concerning decontamination if caught in the midst of an incident. In most cases it would not be necessary to evacuate an NGO team from a country as staff can usually relocate outside a contaminated area. In the case of biological contamination, local authorities may prevent relocation through quarantine restrictions. The hibernation period could range from seven to 28 days depending on the biological agent.

An incident map of recent past and current incidents could be maintained in collaboration with other humanitarian organizations.

Decision-making protocols for provision of humanitarian assistance to beneficiary populations would require knowledge of local community response capabilities and capacities to assist the beneficiary population, and the need for and extent of any international assistance.

Information coordination mechanisms

Major civil emergency management at the tactical level should incorporate integrated emergency management and coordination. This might entail gathering information on the local environment and knowledge of the availability of resources to respond to a chemical, biological or radiological incident, because NGOs will not have fully independent capability in a CBRNE incident. For pre-identification of reliable and credible information sources, it is important to have knowledge of which organizations have the specialized training and capability to operate in a CBRNE risk environment, and what their role, technical capability and capacity would be as a part of an international relief effort.

For staff working in high-risk priority areas, every opportunity should be taken to identify and coordinate with the proper local, national and international public health protection and response authorities and organizations to ensure the highest level of staff and beneficiary safety. Information collection will involve close coordination with international networks and local, regional and national aid structures and other NGOs active in the area. It would also require understanding of the responsibilities, capabilities and limitations of potential first-responder organizations and services in the local context. In many cases, the only reliable CBRNE detection and decontamination equipment might reside with western military or international emergency response organizations, which have response arrangements such as CBRNE and specialist hazardous materials teams to assist with catastrophic incidents in other countries. Links to these capabilities would require formal arrangement through international mechanisms such as foreign offices, NATO, Organisation for the Prohibition of Chemical Weapons, European Community Technical Emergency Response Teams, and the World Health Organization's (WHO's) Chemical and Biological Weapons Team.

In each disaster- or emergency-prone country, the UN Resident Coordinator is responsible for forming and leading a standby UN Disaster Management Team (UNDMT). The team would normally include a core group consisting of the UN Children's Fund (UNICEF), World Food Programme (WFP) and WHO. The team is a mechanism for coordination, providing a forum for information exchange, discussion and consensus seeking. Local and national resources would first be assessed during the initial response intervention to determine the structures and capacity for warning and emergency response. The UNDMT would support the government.

In most countries the government will establish a special ministry or other body charged with overall coordination of government assistance and relations with international organizations. Government requests for international assistance would specify whether any formal or informal request has been made, listed under subheadings of search and rescue, medical teams and supplies, shelter, blankets, clothing, water and sanitation, food items, logistics, communications, repairs to infrastructure, expertise for detailed sector assessment and restoration of critical facilities.

Assistance can be requested through OCHA (UN Office for the Coordination of Humanitarian Affairs), Environmental Emergencies Section, using the Environmental Emergency Notification/Request for International Assistance. This is a standardized format indicating details surrounding the location and emergency type, and the responses planned and undertaken for any national disaster with environmental impacts, and technological, chemical or industrial accidents.

UN assistance is likely to be in the form of emergency relief such as medical/healthcare, food supplies, nutrition, epidemiology, water supplies, hygiene, environment sanitation, emergency shelter, relief materials, construction equipment, communications and logistics systems and facilities.

Technical expertise

As a preparedness measure it would be wise to ensure access to technical expertise. National and international NGOs could draw on organizations with a 24 hour contact line to seek advice and information on incidents relating to public health, infectious diseases, toxicology, radiation and nuclear medicine. In some situations the necessary links may have to be created; in others it may be useful to strengthen existing coordination.

See Resource IX, *Directory of organizations and conventions* for information on key agencies with an information and advisory role on CBRNE incidents.

CHAPTER 3
Field staff safety

Incident emergency response

Warning signs of an attack or incident

USA Advisory System Threat Assessment via multidisciplinary sources would use the following security level alerts:

Severe	Red
High	Amber
Elevated	Yellow
Guarded	Blue
Low	Pale green

Other western countries may have different advisory systems, security alert levels and colour coding, but in middle- or low-income countries there may be no alert or warning system.

> **Be aware that CBRNE incidents can occur without a warning alert or immediate detection of a toxic or dangerous hazard.**

Event recognition

CBRNE hazards are not recognizable by the senses alone. Many chemical agents are odourless and colourless, and some cause no clearly noticeable symptoms (see Chapter 7, *Key chemical agents*).

In the case of a biological agent, the onset of symptoms requires days to weeks to detect and confirm the type of disease outbreak. Surges and triggers of symptoms might ring alarm bells, such as a sudden outbreak of a disease out of context or an unusual disease previously eradicated, and there are a range of other indicators for emerging infectious diseases (see Chapter 8, *Key biological agents*).

In a radiological or nuclear incident radiation is invisible, odourless and tasteless. Exposure indicators may not be immediately apparent due to delayed onset of symptoms (see Chapter 9, *Radiation and nuclear incidents*).

Explosive devices might easily be detected by the discovery of suspicious packages or vehicles, or unusual metal debris or munitions-like material, but they can also be used in concealed covert attacks by suicide bombers (see Chapter 10).

Indicators of an incident might be:

- multiple victims
- casualties displaying symptoms of nausea, breathing difficulty, convulsions and disorientation
- birds and insects dropping from the sky
- unusual dead or dying animals or insects in the area
- unusual liquid, spray, powder or vapour
- droplets or oily film on surfaces
- unexplained odours (bitter almonds, peach kernels, newly mown hay or green grass)
- unusual or unauthorized spraying in the area
- smell and signs of smoke or explosives
- receipt of suspicious mail or packages with odours or white powder.

Risk assessment and staff safety

Safety and protection measures

If and when a CBRNE incident occurs, it is important to know the immediate measures to take:

- **safety**: assess life safety issues
- **protection**: consider how humanitarian organizations can decrease the risk of contamination of their staff
- **risks**: be aware of the effects of exposure and the danger of providing assistance to victims before decontamination has taken place.

In a chemical, radiation or nuclear incident, NGOs should not think of assisting in a potentially contaminated zone (i.e. hot and warm zones) because of the lethality and severe health effects of certain agents and hazards (see Figure 4.1). In the event of an incident involving a persistent chemical agent or radiological/nuclear device found in the vicinity of an NGO project or programme, safety and security issues would have to be considered as to whether to:

- evacuate or shelter in-place (the present locality)
- close, suspend or relocate a project or programme to a safe location
- advise essential staff only to remain on the fringe of the affected area.

Survival and escape kits

Prepare 'escape rucksacks' with essential protective clothing and equipment, including a poncho (or adapted plastic bin bag), face gas mask, butyl gloves and chemical detector paper. Backpacks or grab bags should be with staff at all times, or within easy reach.

Donning (putting on) and doffing (taking off) of an escape kit should only be carried out together with another person, working in pairs, as assistance will be needed with health and safety checks and washing of the protective clothing and equipment (see Resource II, *Personal protective equipment*).

Emergency measures for evacuation

In a major incident, the first consideration of an NGO would have to be protection of field staff and possible escape to a safe refuge/building in a non-contaminated, non-combat area. In high-risk areas each country office contingency plan should include measures for remaining in-place and preparing a safe room (see Box 3.1).

When sheltering in a safe room, listen to the local radio for situation updates. Staff should remain in the safe area until the suspected contamination has been identified and appropriate measures taken to allow safe re-entry or relocation. Wait for rescue, or an 'all clear' communication to go outdoors.

Staff protection principles and safe practice measures for own survival

- One member of security and one of medical staff should be contactable 24 hours a day.

- Everybody should accept the authority of the security officer.

- Staff should never be alone.

- If the hazard type is unknown, assume a worst-case scenario and at-risk environment and put on personal protective clothing.

Escape by foot

If caught on foot in a major chemical incident in the hot zone, initial individual response actions should be taken to avoid becoming a casualty oneself and hence unable to assist others.

- Ensure your own life safety, and protection of critical systems (airways).

- If at hand, put on PPE (a face mask with active carbon and particulate filter to reduce inhalation dosage, or face shield and hair cover, coverall, gloves and boots). If PPE is not available, immediately cover your nose and mouth with an improvised mask by soaking a clean cloth in water.

- Avoid person-to-person contact.

- Remove heavily contaminated clothing.

- Also remove yourself from danger.

- Stay clear of any hazards.

- Minimize time spent around an ongoing source of exposure.

- Maximize distance from suspected sources of exposure.

Box 3.1 Creation of a safe room

Close and seal all windows and exterior doors in the building with duct tape and plastic sheeting to minimize draughts. Block all keyholes and cracks with cotton wool or wet rags and tape; use a water-soaked cloth to seal gaps under doors.

Shut down air-conditioning vents or flows, fans or central heating systems to prevent circulation. In the centre of the building on an upstairs floor (highest level) select an inner room with the least number of windows and doors and, if possible, with access to a bathroom.

As toxic chemical substances such as chlorine are heavier than air, never hide in cellars or trenches. In the case of a radiological dispersal device, take shelter in a building with thick walls, if possible below ground level.

Glass, concrete, metal and other materials will help shield you from radiation.

Safe haven equipment would ideally include:

Waterproof clothing, long-sleeved shirts, long trousers, raincoats, boots, butyl rubber gloves	☐
Several weeks' supply of non-perishable food in sealed containers, and water (3 gallons per person)	☐
Communication equipment, hand-held radio, mobile phone, maps of the local region with designated evacuation routes	☐
(NB Keep important items – computers and documents – in sealed plastic bags)	☐
Torch, candles, battery-operated radio, extra batteries, fire extinguisher	☐
First-aid kit and medicines, soap, household bleach, rubbish bags	☐
Duct tape, plastic sheeting, extra blankets, can or bottle opener, knife and scissors.	☐

- Do not rush in to help, first rethink your initial impulse.

- Do not attempt to go to the aid of victims in the hot contaminated zone.

- If necessary, identify structures for medical evacuation.

- Evacuate the hazardous area if so instructed by emergency responders and collect information at the scene as you evacuate.

- The evacuation should take account of the main wind direction when identifying routes of escape or places of reception.

- Stay clear of fire, smoke and vapour clouds. Be aware that wind conditions can cause the danger zone to shift, e.g. the toxic plume from a chemical release or an explosive incident.

- Run in the opposite wind direction, i.e. upwind from the source, if its location is known, or away from the plume of gas or smoke.

- Identify and ensure a safe distance of 400 metres minimum (1300 feet) from the current or potential contaminated hot hazard zone.

Escape by vehicle

If this would be the most appropriate response during a major hazardous chemical agent release (see Chapter 7, *Key chemical agents* for types and effects):

- Vehicles should be available and equipped for emergency evacuation at all times.

- In a vehicle (if gas has not entered) shut off outside air-intake vents and air conditioning, and close windows.

- Identify potential escape routes and procedures.

- Do not linger for others to join you.

- Accept the fact that you may not be able to help other people at this stage.

- Assess the wind direction (a flag should be attached to each vehicle).

- Immediately drive 5 miles upwind and re-assess the situation.

- Send a radio warning report to base, and listen for further information.

- Do not re-enter the contaminated zone until the all-clear is given.

Re-entry

As per the NGO security guidelines, the decision to re-enter a country following an evacuation after a major incident would generally be made by the operations manager in consultation with the country manager, and based on an all-clear notice from a reliable source.

Similarly, the decision to re-enter a post-incident site following relocation in country would be made by the country manager in consultation with project coordinators and head office. In each circumstance, these decisions should also be based on liaison with local emergency response organizations.

chapter three

Individual emergency decontamination

Individual emergency decontamination of all staff is recommended in the event of suspected exposure to chemical substances. Coordinators should ensure staff members know the simple methods of personal decontamination, and have necessary materials in each safe room, residence or office.

Self-decontamination procedures should be carried out to cleanse the whole body of existing exposure to chemical contaminants or radiation particles.

Box 3.2   Personal decontamination

Personal decontamination materials

- Shower or bucket, soap (liquid if possible), water, sponge or soft brush and chlorine.
- Clean change of clothing.
- Rubbish bags and labels for contaminated clothing and items.

Individual decontamination procedures

- Immediately wipe face and repeatedly flush eyes with large amounts of clean water.
- Remove all contaminated clothing carefully so as not to spread any particles on to the face or skin, place in a plastic bag and seal.
- Use the 'rinse–wipe–rinse' method: wash the entire body from top to toe, including hair, with a mild body soap solution and a secure water source – a shower would be ideal.
- If you have little water, sprinkle talcum powder or flour on the affected skin area, wait 30 seconds, then brush off with a rag or gauze pad; use rubber butyl gloves if available.
- Put on clean clothing.
- Option for a 'worst-case scenario' lacking soap and water or Fullers Earth would be to rub dry earth into clothing to absorb the contaminant, or take clothes off and roll around in the dirt, then wash and change clothing as possible.
- It is best to destroy heavily contaminated clothing by incineration if possible. Items with minimal contamination can be washed in hot water.

CHAPTER 4

Operation management

Planning assumptions

The following assumptions are made for the purpose of this sourcebook.

- National authorities have the primary duty and responsibility for the care and well-being of their citizens and internally displaced people, but do not necessarily execute this duty or have adequate capacity.

- The government of a stricken state bears primary responsibility for disaster assessment, but national and local authorities may not have the capacity or ability to cope effectively with the magnitude or type of response required.

- The UN system or other international or multilateral organizations may provide support as requested or required by the stricken state.

- Liaison, collaboration and on-scene coordination with existing local emergency responders, relevant national authorities and other organizations would be necessary.

- Liaison, based on humanitarian principles, is acceptable to gather security information from military intelligence sources at headquarters and field levels.

Field response procedures

Preparedness and contingency measures

Planning a humanitarian intervention will involve identification of the capacity and preparedness of first responders and civil emergency response organizations involved in search and rescue and containment of hazardous materials incidents.

A local fire brigade, emergency medical or ambulance service, and law enforcement agency would carry out initial emergency response actions in most western industrialized countries, but such services may not be available or adequately equipped or trained in low-income countries.

Technical support

Preparedness includes availability of and access to:

- NGO's emergency response plan
- CBRNE guidelines, technical action cards, incident reporting forms
- Personal protective equipment (PPE)
- Medical protocols for chemical and biological agents
- Medical kits, and access or referral procedures to obtain vaccines or antidotes which may be stockpiled by the Ministry of Health or international health organizations.
  (See also Resources II, III, IV and VI.)

Resources for humanitarian intervention

One preparedness measure would be for an NGO field office to determine local human resources/personnel availability and specialization in various sectors:

- health, medical and clinical –

  diagnostic, triage, treatment, primary care, secondary care

- non-medical –

  operations

  security

  logistics

  water and sanitation

  relief distribution

  satellite communications

  psychosocial support.

Systems for operations

Non-governmental organizations should consider the following operational aspects:

- communication lines – responsibilities and procedures
- logistics supply chain for buffer stocks and vital programme supplies
- procurement – ensure clarity and specification in field requests, procure locally where possible, and import restrictions on certain types of equipment
- water and sanitation equipment and safety measures for decontamination
- transportation routes – roads, railways or airports may be damaged or inaccessible
- asset management – storage (protection of commodities while in transit and on arrival) and distribution of goods and services (maintenance of secure supplies and safeguarding against losses and contamination).

Incident response phase

Civilian population alert

During a major incident, there should be some official means to alert the affected population of the situation and to instruct them on the best forms of prevention or protective measures, such as evacuation or shelter in-place.

Channels of communication in middle- and low-income countries might be a combination of loudspeaker, TV and/or radio announcements. Alerting the civilian population to an incident is likely to cause mass movement, fear and panic – which could possibly be more dangerous than the event itself. Any alerts or warnings must be coordinated with the local authorities – good links should have been established beforehand with these authorities.

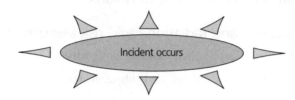

Scene safety and security by first emergency responders

The **Scene Safety Rule** provides a useful method to assess levels of 'safe' access and safety for responses to incidents where the cause is unknown:

- **Step 1** – **one** casualty: approach with caution. Provision of normal procedures for first aid and medical treatment.

- **Step 2** – **two** casualties: approach with caution and consider all options.

- **Step 3** – **three or more** casualties: do not approach the scene. Withdraw. Contain. Report. Isolate yourself. Send for specialist help. Do not compromise your safety or that of others.

Incident response procedures

Trained first responders should follow safe approach procedures and take special precautions: wear full PPE and treat as 'an incident with deliberate or accidental release' as the type of chemical agent or kind of dispersal device may not be known:

- approach the incident upwind and at a safe distance: 100–600 metres depending on the type of hazard

- observe unusual signs and toxic cloud formation

- conduct rapid scene assessment and report findings.

Scene/incident report

Reporting actions of first emergency responders should include essential information. CHALETS is a useful reporting aid:

- **Casualties** – approximate number of dead, injured and uninjured persons
- **Hazards** – present and potential
- **Access and exit** – best access routes for emergency vehicles and responders
- **Location** – exact location of incident
- **Emergency services** – present and required
- **Type of incident** – brief details
- **Safety** – ensure safety of everyone in the vicinity.

Chemical, biological and radiation rapid risk assessment

This should always be based on the following framework:

- **Source** – the agent(s) involved and their physical state
- **Pathway** – potential route(s) of exposure
- **Receptor** – population at risk.

Emergency services should assess conditions that can increase or decrease contamination, such as meteorological information on current weather and wind direction and force.

Incident command control and coordination, comprising a management team, may be established where multiple agencies are involved in responding to large-scale disasters.

Zones for emergency response operations

The procedures below describe a sequence of best practice actions and functions that should ideally be taken by emergency response personnel (trained for rescue, site security, hazard control and containment, decontamination, emergency medical aid – if available with sufficient capability and capacity). Different levels of PPE should be worn according to the type of hazard or agent, specific function, and zone of operation (see Resource II, *Personal protective equipment*).

On arrival at an incident scene, a first priority would be to determine and mark perimeters for exclusion zones, called cordons:

1 **inner zone** to limit immediate danger of the hazard, contaminant or exposure = **hot zone**

2 **contamination reduction area** for decontamination and life saving treatment = **warm zone**

3 **outer zone** for support: triage, first aid and referral = **cold zone**.

Incident scene security should restrict unauthorized movement into the hot and warm zones, and monitor entry and exit control points.

Security and crowd management should ensure public health and safety precautions.

The hot, warm and cold zone functions are as follows.

HOT ZONE = **high risk and danger area**

- **Exclusion area**: 100 metres. Entry only for **frontline emergency responders** with gas-tight suits and self-contained breathing apparatus: **full PPE (level A)**.

- Victims caught in the hazard zone with risk of contamination from toxic and lethal chemicals, radiation exposure, detonation of an explosive device, collapse of buildings or other dangerous hazard.

- Response personnel for hot zone activities will be **specially trained rescuers** for CBRNE agents, hazardous materials and emergency decontamination.

- **Detection, monitoring, hazard control and containment operations** would require only specially trained and fully PPE-equipped first responders.

- **Initial rescue actions** would involve:
  - emergency decontamination of the face of the victim
  - basic life-saving medical care – airway support, cervical spine support, haemorrhage and seizure control
  - evacuation of injured and potential victims in adjacent areas from the danger zone to the warm zone (to await full decontamination).

An **exit and transfer point** should be set up leading to the:

WARM ZONE = **contamination-reduction area** on the fringe, located uphill and upwind from the hot zone – likely to contain contaminated victims but is an **area out of immediate danger** of the hazardous material. A safe approach for hazardous materials would be located approximately 400 metres from the hazard site. Rescue and treatment activities in this zone would be as follows.

- **Mass or gross decontamination** of people and rescue vehicles, requiring emergency response personnel to wear **level B or level C PPE respirators** to protect against the risk of cross-contamination by casualties off-gassing.

- **Initial triage** specific to the agent and syndrome to:
  - identify people most at risk (unconscious, injured and burns casualties)
  - prioritize cases for treatment
  - identify casualties who need referral to the most appropriate health structure (e.g. isolation unit, hospital with quarantine/observation units, medical and surgical departments, mobile field hospital)
  - give emergency first aid (open airway, but **do not attempt mouth-to-mouth resuscitation on victims**).

Casualty decontamination for **walking casualties** and/or **contaminated individuals** who should be moved from the triage area to the decontamination point, where clothing removal and decontamination should take place (using rinse–wipe–rinse method with liquid soap and water).

Emergency medical treatment: appropriate measures according to the type of agent, syndrome or injuries.

The casualty or person should cross the decontamination line which separates the warm zone from the cold zone.

COLD ZONE = support zone (outer zone)

Out-of-danger area and **non-contaminated zone** – clean or clear from the initial hazard.

This is the furthest boundary of the incident area, and provides a safe location to deploy emergency measures and treat victims. Most medical response activities would be in the cold zone, where **more definitive triage** and **first aid** are carried out prior to referral to hospitals or health facilities.

(Para)medic responders need to wear the equivalent of **level C PPE** for life support, more sophisticated airway support, circulatory support, covering of open wounds or administration of antidotes for chemical poisoning. Once casualties are stabilized and decontaminated they may be transported to a hospital or health facility.

Humanitarian assistance can be carried out in the cold zone (check first if all people have been decontaminated, if affected by a contaminated hazard).

ENTERING

People outside the contaminated zone, unknowingly moving towards the affected area, should be instructed to move back to a safe or clean area.

Medical assistance and casualty management

Key principles

The key principles of casualty management are provision of basic life support treatment, and 'do the best for the most'. This may mean having to leave casualties at the scene in a heavily mass-casualty, high-impact, hazardous incident.

Decontamination

Decontamination of chemical casualties will be essential before any attempt to treat victims. If in doubt, assume that the agent is persistent, with a possibility of off-gassing and risk to the respiratory system or of skin absorption. Strip clothing (with cultural sensitivity), wash the exposed area using the rinse–wipe–rinse method, and cover with clean clothing or some kind of protective material to avoid hypothermia.

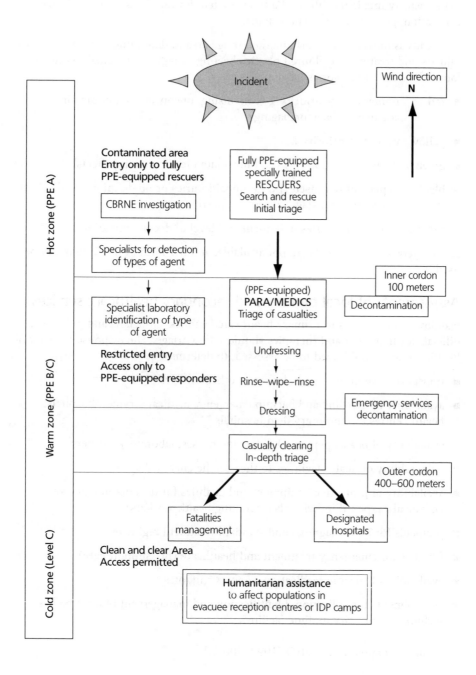

Figure 4.1 First responder zones. (Source: adapted from Home Office, 2003.)

Triage system

Mass casualty incidents will need a triage system for rapid assessment of a patient's respiration, perfusion and mental status.

A casualty is moved to a clearly marked triage area to determine priority of critical injuries and treatment. Coloured plastic sheeting or tags are assigned to one of four colour-coded categories labelled:

- **red** **immediate** = **priority 1** (convulsing, unconscious, not breathing adequately, haemorrhaging)

- **yellow** **urgent** = **priority 2**

- **green** **delayed** = **priority 3** (no immediate life-threatening effects)

- **black** **expectant/deceased** (pre-terminal injuries or no definitive medical care at pre-hospital stage, except supportive care).

Triage tags would list injuries, treatment and level of decontamination.

In an emergency where tags are not available, another form of marking might be used.

Assessments of local primary and secondary healthcare services

Handover of casualties to primary healthcare facilities, clinicians and public health officials for treatment and therapies should follow triage. The response capacity of health services would need to be assessed, to determine:

- transport capabilities – ambulances or other vehicles

- availability of first-line and backup emergency medical services, hospitals, health centres or temporary field hospitals

- availability of health personnel – doctors, nurses, laboratory workers

- vulnerability of health facilities to the specific chemical agent

- availability of protective equipment and facilities for decontamination of chemically exposed individuals (including health workers)

- protocols for clear diagnosis and standard treatment regimens

- facilities for emergency treatment and healthcare (life-support care)

- availability of specific medication, such as antidotes

- arrangements for collection, identification and management of dead bodies, including temporary morgue facilities.

[Source: Adapted from WHO (1999, 2003).]

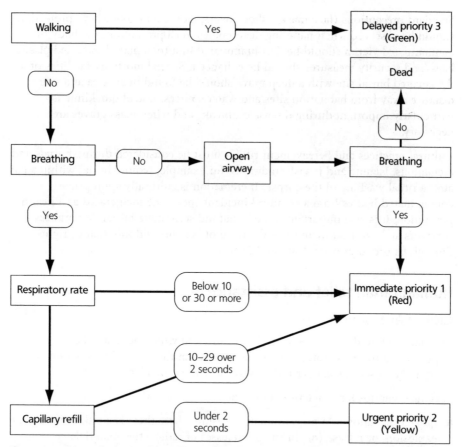

If you are unable to obtain a capillary refill and the pulse is over 120 beats per minute then the patient is **priority 1**.

Figure 4.2   The adult triage sieve. (Source: Hodgetts and Mackway-Jones, 1995.)

Distribution and administration of mass countermeasures

A confirmed outbreak of smallpox, for example, would require vaccines to be administered. This would require:

- locations and setup of a cold-chain system and distribution points
- triage and screening for contraindications
- medical protocols for recommended dosage of drugs
- records and medical cards or stamp.

Environmental health – burials

All deceased bodies affected by a CBRNE incident should be considered a potential health risk, and should be protected from disease vectors such as rats.

Standard precautions (face masks, shoe covers, gloves and gowns, eye protection) should be observed when handling dead bodies. As a precaution, the body of a contaminated victim should be decontaminated first then placed in sealed plastic bags, and security measures should be enhanced. Special mortuary facilities or a demarcated burial site with a deep grave should be found in an area at a safe distance away from habitation sites and water sources. Use of quicklime is particularly important during disease outbreaks and when mass graves are necessary.

Cultural practices and bereavement rituals must be considered during burials and cremations. Islamic and Jewish traditions, for example, require burial within a day after a ritual washing of the corpse. If cremation is culturally appropriate, contaminated bodies from a chemical incident should be incinerated as a health precaution. It is also important to note that indiscriminate burial demoralizes the survivors and can lead them to be deprived of benefits and inheritance rights through failure to provide death certificates.

Humanitarian relief and assistance

Civilian evacuation

Evacuation should be a measure of last resort, and would generally be implemented by law enforcement authorities when the affected population is likely to be in serious danger if they stay close to an incident site.

Specific scenarios for evacuation might be:

- quick evacuation as a precautionary measure where there is a risk of imminent explosion, or release (or threatened release) of radioactive materials

- spontaneous evacuation during an incident where there is spread of fire, or continuation of a hazardous release over a prolonged period, or threat of attack

- post-incident – in the event of gross environmental contamination.

The affected population should have warning on:

- the extent of the evacuation area

- the proposed destination for evacuees

- whether transport is needed and available

- what support organizations would be available for wayside assistance.

NGO operation management actions

Security personnel in NGOs should try immediately to notify field management, who should take appropriate action to:

- alert field staff and account for all employees

- assess the risk to staff, beneficiary groups, utilities and assets
- determine operational and incident priorities, and consult headquarters
- establish an emergency operations control and coordination base
- activate an emergency communication system
- gather information from relevant sources, including meteorological conditions
- keep a record of decisions and actions.

Hazard information gathering

At the outset of an emergency situation, where NGOs are outside the affected area in the safe zone, information could be sought from relevant authorities and organizations to determine: what has happened, where the perimeter of the incident is, the severity of injury of casualties, the amount of damage, and which emergency organizations are responding to the incident to stabilize and identify the hazard and provide rescue and first aid to civilian casualties.

Information for assessment

Decision-making on potential NGO involvement in a humanitarian emergency should be based on a range of questions (Box 4.1 overleaf).

Box 4.1 Disaster assessment

General information

- Type of disaster incident?

- Likely secondary hazards (fire, release of toxic substances) in the affected area?

- What is affected?

- Does the NGO have any programmes in the affected area? If so, what are they and where?

- What are the current and forecasted local weather conditions? (Meteorological conditions: temperature, wind direction, wind speed, rainfall, sunshine, cloud.)

- What are the geographical characteristics? (Valleys, mountains, lakes, other waters, size in km^2.)

- Estimated total population in the affected area?

- Population density/settlement pattern in that area?

- Has the government formally requested international assistance (or is it likely to?)

- Is cooperation with neighbouring areas or countries foreseeable?

- What kind of humanitarian assistance is requested?

- Will the local authorities facilitate humanitarian aid?

- What are the capabilities and capacities of the affected country medical services?

- How vulnerable are the victims?

- Is ready access to the victims possible?

Initial estimate of impacts

Population affected

- Estimated number of individuals and residential buildings close to the release?

- How many reported: deaths, injured, displaced or homeless?

- Estimated men, women, children affected?

- What medical conditions has the incident caused?

- What is the situation of those affected: coping mechanisms?

Public health

■ What diseases are endemic, any outbreaks reported?

■ What was the health of the population before the incident?

■ What percentage of hospitals are functioning, and the capacity of these?

Water and sanitation

■ Any effects on water supply, waste disposal, availability of drinking water?

Transport infrastructure

■ What means of access to affected areas?

■ Which is the nearest functioning airport(s) and what is their handling capability?

Communication and power supply

■ What are the impacts on power supply?

■ Do local facilities (hospitals/water-pumping stations) have backup generators?

■ Are landlines/mobile phones functioning?

Search and rescue

■ Has the incident caused structural collapse?

■ What type of structures collapsed (hospitals, schools, government buildings, multi-storey housing units)?

■ Are local authorities requesting assistance with search and rescue?

■ Who is conducting/coordinating the present rescue effort and for how long has this been under way?

Box 4.2   **Disaster response**

Information on initial responses

Assessments

■ What assessments have been made/planned? By whom, what outcome?

Government response

■ What has been the government response so far?

■ Which is the lead government ministry/body?

■ Is there a well established in-country emergency response mechanism?

■ What is the role of other relevant structures (emergency committee, civil defence)?

■ What are the capabilities of the above to respond?

Other responses

■ What is the response of the humanitarian community (UN, Red Cross/Red Crescent Societies, donors, NGOs, others)?

■ What are the capabilities and capacities of those responding?

■ What are the gaps (medicines, water, shelter, clothing)?

■ Which is the lead UN agency?

■ Is the UN OCHA Disaster Management Team (UNDMT) present?

■ Have they met; is a disaster plan in place; has it been activated?

■ Have any situation reports been issued? Has any other information been shared?

Coordination

■ What coordination structures are in place for the incident (government/UN/local community)?

Factors affecting response

■ What is the security situation? Is the incident site(s) safe for personnel to operate in?

■ What other country-specific factors may affect response?

■ How is the situation being reported in the local and national media? Are they reliable?

Disaster relief priorities

To provide essential relief items for the affected population, an assessment of needs and priorities should be made (Box 4.3).

> #### Box 4.3 Relief and medical supplies
>
> - What are the priorities?
> - What are the likely personnel requirements?
> - How will medical supplies be transported to their destination?
> - How will medical supplies be controlled and stored at the destination?
> - Expected timing and rate of use of distribution?
> - Speed of delivery possible from local resources?
> - Appropriateness of items available, and quality?
> - Likely effects on the local market?

chapter four

Safe site planning for displaced people

Voluntary agencies may be required to assist with activities to support displaced people who are spontaneous or organized evacuees. This may involve setting up different structures to cater for various needs and provision, including:

- setup of survivor reception centre and utilities
- provision of temporary extensions or tented structures as health buildings
- medical and primary healthcare of injured or ill evacuees
- special needs of vulnerable people, e.g. children, elderly and disabled people
- setup and instruction in secondary decontamination of affected people.

In planning emergency treatment sites for people evacuated or displaced from the incident scene, weather and natural resource conditions should be considered.

Safe location

It would be important to note prevailing weather conditions and forecasts. If the wind always comes from one direction, evacuation should essentially take place to a 'safe distance' from the impact zone: a minimum of 5–10 km from a chemical agent release site, and a minimum of 30 km from a nuclear explosion site. In setting up a reception centre, temporary hospital or health structure, the site location should be upwind of the hazard, agent release or cloud plume.

Safe water source

If using river water, a place should be chosen upstream and upwind of the incident location. An expert water organization should be used to test the water for contamination, and availability of a safe water supply for consumption (minimum 20 litres per person per day) should be ensured, if possible.

Civilian decontamination guidance

There may be situations where people affected by a chemical incident flee the scene to seek safe refuge. Where local emergency responders are not available, it would be necessary to convey the importance of adequate decontamination so that people do not risk spreading potential contamination to others in the clean area. Cultural and religious issues should be addressed, for example by provision of separate facilities for derobing, bathing, and dressing in temporary clothing or blankets.

The decontamination process would consist of guidance or instruction to contaminated persons from a safe distance, perhaps using traditional leaders or community representative as intermediaries. (See Resource V, *Decontamination procedures* for more detail.)

Emergency relief and logistics

Humanitarian aid organizations should assess the resource needs of the affected displaced population in cooperation with local authorities. Consideration should also be given to the possible effect a major incident might have on procurement of supplies and logistics chains, and the implications of using scarce resources to meet short-term needs.

Health resources and medical supplies

Medical supplies and antidotes might be obtained from the national health authority, which can request additional supplies from the international body involved in the incident response, for example WHO, Centers for Disease Control and Prevention (CDC), or the Organisation for the Prohibition of Chemical Weapons (OPCW). Medical personnel should consult the relevant medical protocols for chemical agents and biowarfare agents in the Resources section of this sourcebook.

Other kinds of assistance may also be needed, for example:

- provision of supportive care (oxygen and intubation) and care for secondary effects (wounds, injuries and infection)

- nutrition – additional supplies of food for quarantined and isolated casualties or evacuees and internally displaced people

- psychosocial support for people suffering mental trauma and anxiety post-incident.

> ## Box 4.4 Resource needs assessment
>
> - **Shelter** for physical protection and safe place to shield from exposure – tents that are easily collapsible and portable may be the only option in a non-built-up area.
>
> - **Water** – quantity requirements and delivery mode (tankers, bladders, hosepipes, sprinkler systems) for gross decontamination use and safe water consumption. The location of additional or alternative water supplies or source would need to be identified and made accessible within a short distance and time for a decontamination process to begin. It may be a question of whether safe water can be trucked to the decontamination site and distributed in a practical way.
>
> - **Equipment** – buckets, brushes, hygiene packs, sponges, towels, soap.
>
> - **Fresh clothing** for contaminated people to change into.
>
> - **Sanitation** for contaminated waste disposal (on waste ground).
>
> - **Health** – primary healthcare and mental health capacity (support existing primary healthcare systems and hospital facilities).
>
> - **Food** – procurement and distribution systems (draw on local resources and voluntary organizations).

International stockpiles might be drawn upon from UN agencies:

- WHO stockpiles of medical supplies, logistical equipment and communication equipment

- WFP strategic stocks of food and equipment

- UNICEF 'ready-to-use' basic kits, communication equipment, security equipment

- UNHCR (Office of the UN High Commissioner for Refugees) 'service packages' of self-contained facilities.

Coordination of humanitarian organizations

Coordination between different entities responsible for providing humanitarian assistance can ensure systematic coverage and complementarity, avoiding duplication of roles and provision. Coordination steps might involve:

- setup of communication channels with the relevant national authorities and, if appropriate, the CIMIC Officer of field military units, to seek information on the security situation and identification of the type of agent or device, and impact

- planning of components for heightened security communications and logistics

- linkage into coordination mechanisms between national, regional and local emergency relief sectors of health, logistics, transport services, water and sanitation providers
- identification of roles and responsibilities among agencies for rapid response and capacity to carry out decontamination, possibly with small multi-agency teams of frontline workers specially equipped to operate
- registration of NGO specialist capability for coordination with national, UN, multilateral and international organizations:
  - UN Humanitarian Coordinator and UN OCHA Disaster Assessment and Coordination (UNDAC) team's On-Site Operations and Coordination Centre for technical emergencies
  - OPCW Advanced Coordination and Assessment Team (ACAT) for chemical emergencies
  - WHO for either biological, chemical or radiological advice and support
  - WHO/CDC/specialist laboratory on-site representatives for sampling, or satellite communications to advisory public health hotlines
  - UN Security Coordinator (UNSECOORD), UN Development Programme (UNDP) and UNHCR for field security briefings
  - EU Civil Protection Programme, which aims to reinforce cooperation in civil protection and health; reduce the vulnerability of the population through preventive measures; mitigate the consequences of an attack and facilitate the return to normal conditions; and cooperate with third and international organizations and coordination with the European Council and European Commission.

The advantage of a coordination structure is that it puts together a variety of necessary skills which none of the agencies alone could build up efficiently.

(See Resource IX, *Directory of organizations and conventions.*)

CHAPTER 5

Psychosocial support

Biological and chemical weapons have been used in warfare for many generations. They are relatively easy to produce and quite effective. They instil intense fear and may cause large-scale casualties. The idea of becoming ill through 'undetectable' agents is very frightening. It touches deeply a very basic human need for control and predictability. Consequently, the emotions triggered by the threat (let alone the use) of these types of weapon are often irrational and extremely strong. When threatened with or experiencing the use of chemical and biological weapons, the psychosocial side effects – fear, social disruption and economic downturn – are often the most prominent.

The long-term consequence of exposure to a mild dose of chemical and biological weapons is an area that requires more research. The lack of knowledge and awareness further contributes to the psychological impact of this type of weapon.

Chemical and biological threat

A threat of chemical or biological weapons often results in profound excitation among both authorities and civilian population. This naturally results in increased alertness and implementation of monitoring, preparedness and prevention activities. The whole atmosphere of threat and alertness may result in serious social disruption (rumour, chaos, scapegoating, paranoia, denial, aggression) and/or augmented health complaints (misinterpretation of bodily signs, somatization, stress-related complaints).

In situations of both threat and use of chemical or biological weapons, panic seriously impairs effective interventions. Although experience shows that people generally react in a cooperative and adaptive way, panic-prevention mechanisms are important: providing structured and consistent information; building relationships of trust with leaders; and involving the host community in composing and conveying information.

Post-attack

Hot or warm zones directly affected by chemical and biological weapons or agents would require detection, identification, diagnosis and protection equipment that is generally only available for trained first emergency responders and military staff. The lack of knowledge of the physical and psychological consequences of exposure to lethal chemical and biological agents would make NGO managers reluctant to expose staff to such an environment.

The phase of the emergency defines the content of the mental health intervention. Various phases and activities are described in Table 5.2. The activities implemented would depend (essentially) on the ongoing assessment of security and on proximity to the chemical agent.

After an attack with chemical or biological agents, psychobiological reactions are likely to become manifest. Rapid, accurate triage and effective treatment (including containment strategies) are essential to cover the direct psychiatric and psychological consequences of exposure to agents (disorientation, depersonalization, hallucinations, delirium).

To make an accurate diagnosis and intervention, it is essential to realize that some biological agents have specific psychiatric/psychological effects (Table 5.1).

Syndromes

Table 5.1   Neuro-psychiatric syndromes or symptoms caused by biological agents

Agent	Syndrome/symptoms	Comment
Anthrax	Meningitis	May be rapidly progressive
Brucellosis	Depression, irritability, headaches, malaise, fatigue	Fatalities associated with central nervous system in one-third of patients
Q fever	Encephalitis, hallucinations	In advanced cases
Botulinum toxin	Depression	Due to lengthy recovery
Viral encephalitis	Depression, cognitive impairment	Other mood changes also reported
All biological agents	Delirium	Acutely impaired attention, memory and perceptual disturbances

Exposure to chemical or biological weapons may also trigger psychological or psychiatric complaints that are not directly related to the chemical or biological attack (e.g. acute/traumatic stress, psychosis, shock, anxiety/panic disorder, and unclear psychological signs as a result of attention-seeking behaviour). Awareness of suspected exposure to radiological hazards could carry even more psychological elements.

Finally, all types of psychosocial problems may emerge. The increased general stress and its misinterpretation (e.g. autonomic arousal being confused with infections or intoxication) can seriously impede the functioning of the healthcare system. Information and education of the general public may be helpful in these circumstances.

Mental health interventions

Table 5.2 Possible mental health interventions in populations affected by chemical and biological warfare

Phase	Intervention
All phases	**Staff care**
	Have clear security and evacuation plans and procedures
	Establish 'helping the helpers' system (peer or professional psychosocial unit)
	Work/rest cycles - enhance observation of masked symptoms and over-dedication
	Rule-governed behaviour during ambiguous situations reduces stress and enhances performance
	Regular, fixed drink breaks to avoid heat casualties
	Suspected low dosage exposure - do not hesitate to send people for treatment immediately
	Create openness and discuss concerns on safety and contamination regularly
	No alcohol in and around working place
	Sensitivity to staff problems, concerns and possible low dose symptoms
	Daily assessment and ongoing security assessment by management
	Panic management
	Compose preparedness plan
	Communication - provide structured, consistent information; build trust relationships with leaders; involve host community in composing and conveying information.
	Implement appropriate public self-protective mechanisms
	Ongoing community education on various health issues
	Consider establishing an information centre
First aid (outreach triage ground)	Brief first responders on security management and on medical and mental health case management
	Bring patients to immediate safety
	Prescription of antipsychotic and anxiolytic medication
	Crisis counselling intervention (containment)
	Stabilize cases with acute traumatic stress
	Inform patients or family regarding normal side effects of drugs
	When possible, involve family members in the care of patients

Table 5.2   Continued.

Phase	Intervention
Second phase (basic healthcare unit)	Prescription of antipsychotic and anxiolytic medication (treatment simple and conservative)
	Crisis counselling intervention (containment)
	Stabilize cases with acute traumatic stress
	Provide time and resources for 'emotional ventilation' (frank and open discussions)
	Focused provision of psycho-education and information
	Involve natural care-givers as patient monitors
	Organize (camp) outreach for medical and psychological cases
Stabilization phase	Run psychosocial programmes used for chronic crisis

Source: de Jong and Prosser (2003)

Staff care

An extra consideration for situations of mass threat or attack of chemical and biological agents is the management of national and expatriate staff.

Programme management must take into account:

- staff safety, which includes control of proximity to chemical agents, and also possible security risks caused by the scarcity of evacuation possibilities or angry reactions of the host community

- staff reactions directly related to the exposure (e.g. impaired concentration and cognitive functioning, disturbances in memory, over-dedication)

- (traumatic) reactions among staff caused by the exposure to panic, and high mortality.

To manage these risks, the programme management must monitor the situation daily and assess the situation themselves, not depending on reports from the field. A 'helping-the-helpers service' must be in place to identify and support staff affected by the direct or indirect consequences of working in areas of chemical and biological warfare.

PART II
HAZARDS

CHAPTER 6

CBRNE hazards

Table 6.1 Key chemical hazards

Hazard	Characteristics, effects, treatment
Likely to involve volatile liquid or substances	**Transmission into the body:** Inhalation, ingestion or penetration/absorption through skin, mucous membranes of the eyes, nose, mouth. Risk of secondary contamination
Persistent: chemical rain or spray aims to contaminate people, equipment or ground	
Non-persistent: toxic vapour cloud over target aims for rapid knockdown and has ability to exploit ground soon after attack	
Airburst borne sprays – weaponized agent with chemical warfare device:	
explosive shell and spray device	
crop-dusting aircraft or pesticide generator	
drone aeroplane with chemical or biological agents	
bomblets or artillery-delivered systems using shells and rockets	
munitions-related release of a nerve agent	
unguided helium balloon	
Nerve gases:	**Nerve agents** are colourless, tasteless, and have a fast rate of action with cumulative effects (lethal)
Soman	
Tabun	Interfere with nerve pathways between brain and muscles
Sarin	
VX	Affect the eyes, nose, mouth, airways; cause nausea, vomiting, tight chest, paralysis in skeletal muscles (arms, legs), airways and gastro-intestinal tract
	Individual mortality high
	Intensive treatment: immediate high dose of atropine and pralidoxime

Blood poison: hydrogen cyanide, lethal dose kills in within 5 minutes

Blood agents: Hydrogen cyanide smells of bitter almonds; absorbed via lungs, eyes, injured skin

Quick action

Causes respiratory paralysis, cardiac arrest

No cure; give supportive treatment - oxygen

Blister agents:

Mustard gas (low mortality rate)

Lewisite (high mortality rate)

Blister agents are damaging casualty agents, mainly non-lethal but can attack skin causing painful, slow-healing blisters and long-term disablement

Characteristics: oily liquids, not water-soluble, evaporate slowly, can contaminate environment for weeks

Symptoms: 4-6 hours/several days, burns, blisters on eyes, lungs, mucous membranes (eyes, nose, mouth), skin.

Treatment: short-term survival good, burn care; decontamination

Choking and irritating gas:

Phosgene

Chlorine

Choking/lung irritant, causes lung oedema (fluid), cold burns

High individual mortality

Treatment: intensive care necessary

Incapacitating:

Adamsite

Carfentanyl

Lofentanyl

Incapacitating agents can cause respiratory problems, vomiting

Can be lethal in major doses

Treat with antidote naloxone (but not for Adamsite)

Riot control:

Tear gas

Riot control agents cause pain, burning, irritation on mucous membranes and skin in minutes, temporary blindness

No long-term effects

Remove to air

Mental incapacitant:

LSD (confusion, hallucinations, psychosis)

Table 6.2   Hazardous industrial chemicals

Hazard	Characteristics and effects
Accidents or deliberate attacks	
Industrial chemical manufacturing plant hazards (chlorine, ammonium nitrate, pesticides, fertilizers, petroleum)	Gas or noxious fumes, chemical mist or vapour
Oil refinery explosion	Inhalation will cause airway irritation, coughing, shortness of breath
Oil or chemical tanker crash or spillage	Direct skin/eye exposure will cause irritation and itching
Petrol station fire	
Major internal fire at industrial site/premises	Burns and trauma, treatment for environmental contamination
Steel works explosion	Power supply breakdown
Freight train derailment with chemical substance cargo	Overwhelming of emergency services
Riverboat transport with chemical cargo	
Natural disaster triggering a chemical leak (floods, earth tremor or earthquake, landslide)	Death, destruction, casualties, possible crush injuries
	Potential chemical or radiation exposure
	Spread of diseases

Table 6.3 Key biological hazards

Hazard	Characteristics, clinical effects, treatment
Transmission mechanisms: crop-dusting aircraft spray tank on a military aircraft – droplet spread aerosol generators – spread occurs through air generating invisible clouds with droplet particles >10 micrometers, area covered varies with wind speed, humidity and sunlight	An intentional airborne release will be undetectable initially until symptomatic disease outbreak occurs Standard precautions – wash hands, wear gloves, mask, eye protection, shoe cover and gown; use alternative ventilation (not mouth-to-mouth)
Bacteria	
Anthrax (can be refined into weapons-grade bacterial spores)	*Anthrax* spores in lungs can cause inhalation anthrax – symptoms of fever, shock, later death. Anthrax vaccine requires multiple inoculations over 7 months for protection (pre-exposure vaccines not recommended for first responders)
Tularaemia (transmitted from small mammals)	*Tularaemia* can lead to pneumonia, chest pain, bloody sputum and breathing difficulties. Requires antibiotic treatment
Plague (pneumonic, bubonic, pulmonary, septicaemia)	*Pneumonic plague*, transmitted person-to-person: coughing, sneezing, inhalation into lungs, droplets spread by hands and touching.
Brucellosis (ingested bacteria from animals: pigs, goats, dogs, cattle)	*Brucellosis:* highly infectious via the airborne route – derived from farm animal aerosols: fever, headache, weakness. Needs special lab tests. Fatalities uncommon. Requires antibiotic treatment
Viruses	
Smallpox (variola major) One confirmed case is a public health emergency	*Smallpox* Highly infectious, no cure (30% fatal) Only prevention through pre- and post-exposure vaccination *Smallpox prophylaxis:* post-exposure vaccine = 95% immunity. Requires hospital admittance, isolation, respiratory protection, barrier nursing, supportive care
Haemorrhagic fever (e.g. Ebola)	*Viral haemorrhagic fevers:* non-communicable disease, but transmission via contact with body fluids. Requires supportive care

cont.

Table 6.3 Key biological hazards *cont.*

Hazard	Characteristics, clinical effects, treatment
Toxins (chemical compounds obtained from biological sources)	**Toxins** may be lethal or incapacitating Rapid in action
Ricin (extracted from castor oil beans), used as an assassination toxin, slow action, high fatality rate	*Ricin* can cause severe, often fatal human disease – requires supportive treatment and intensive care
Botulism	*Botulism* causes muscle weakness and paralysis – requires supportive care and antibiotics (passive immunization)
Aflatoxin	*Aflatoxin* causes skin rashes, respiratory problem weakening, and shock - requires superactivated charcoal if swallowed

Table 6.4 Key radiation and nuclear hazards

Hazard	Characteristics, clinical effects, treatment
Radiation exposure risks Conventional explosives used to disperse radioactive materials 'Dirty bomb' via radiation dispersal device: explosive material (dynamite) attached to radioactive material **Types of nuclear release:** Airburst Surface Subsurface **Nuclear accidents:** Nuclear power plant accidents (Three Mile Island, Chernobyl) Nuclear materials processing plant accidents (Japan) Radioactively contaminated materials, storage, processing facilities mishaps Nuclear waste transport truck or train accidents **Nuclear waste incidents:** (NB 400 Nuclear Reactors in operation around the world) Enriched uranium or other radioactive substances	**A dirty bomb explosion** would disperse radioactive materials into the environment and cause extensive damage **Radiation external exposure risk:** dose of ionizing radiation **Radiation exposure and external contamination:** radioactive material present on patient's body or clothes (possible radiation burns) **Internal contamination:** radioactive material ingested or inhaled by patient or taken into body via wounds **Total or partial body exposure:** with thermal, chemical or radiation burns and/or trauma **Physiological effects** result from exposure to blast (tissue disruption); thermal radiation (burns); ionizing radiation (cell death/changes) Use protective clothing (mask) to prevent transferring contamination Patients present a hazard to rescuers and medical personnel, will need decontamination If life is not directly threatened, decontamination takes precedence: remove all contaminated materials, use long-handled instruments to remove contaminated items, work carefully but quickly, keep distance from patient

cont.

Table 6.4   Key radiation and nuclear hazards *cont.*

Hazard	Characteristics, clinical effects, treatment
Nuclear waste incidents *cont*:	Treat life-threatening conditions
Nuclear waste, spent fuel and radioactive waste	**Burn care:** will require specialist hospital Acute radiation syndrome requires supportive care
Nuclear terrorism: an attack on or sabotage of a nuclear power	
Plant (suicide air crash into nuclear installation)	**Nuclear weapon:** 50% blast and shock 35% thermal radiation
Missile fired into nuclear power plant	10% residual nuclear radiation 4% initial nuclear radiation 1% electromagnetic pulse
Other nuclear hazards and risks:	
Real terrorist atomic bomb detonated – nuclear bomb (mini-nuke) could contain a few kg of plutonium and <20 kg of highly enriched uranium	**Lifeline breakdown/disruption:** Power supply breakdown Water supply contamination Food chain contamination (cobalt 60) Environmental contamination (e.g. plutonium contamination of ground, water, air lasts up to 60 years)
Nuclear power station leak – limited nuclear war overseas, fallout carried by wind	
Illicit trafficking of nuclear/radioactive material worldwide	

Table 6.5   Enhanced high-yield explosive hazards

Hazard	Characteristics, effects, treatment
Airburst weapons	Early warning - birds, insects falling from sky
Surface-to-air missiles	
Cluster bombs (C-bombs) and other submunitions	C-bomb has explosive burster tube inside munition and contains thousands of bomblets
Fuel air bombs (FAE) (Vietnam, Afghanistan)	FAE and thermobaric bombs create a high-pressure searing fireball, massive blast and shock wave; FAE fuels are highly toxic
Thermobaric bomb (vapour reacts explosively with oxygen)	
High-power microwave or electromagnetic bomb (E-bomb) equipment	E-bomb can fry communication links, and damage water distribution systems and hospital technical equipment
Vehicle bomb - deliberate explosion (e.g. use of semtex high-explosive charge, black powder pipe bomb, or remote-detonation devices)	Effects - death, injury, burns, trauma
	Surgery for injuries from blasts (shrapnel) and burns: treatment in special burns units of an acute hospital, trauma treatment, psychosocial support

CHAPTER 7

Key chemical agents

Conventional warning signs of a chemical agent release

Warning signs vary depending on the chemical agent used and the delivery method:

- spraying from low aircraft
- dead animals with no apparent or observable cause of death
- individuals who are experiencing or demonstrating symptoms consistent with chemical exposure.

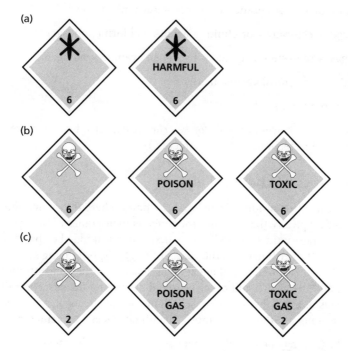

Figure 7.1   Placards associated with hazardous cargo: (a) toxic substances (non-combustible); (b) toxic substances (combustible); (c) gases (toxic and/or corrosive).

Agent detection and verification would require specialist training to explore:

■ type of agent (and identification of the degree of refinement of the chemical)

■ toxicity of the chemical

■ dispersal or transmission mode

■ duration of activity in the environment

■ route, nature and extent of exposure

■ severity of the effect.

Types of chemical agent

To better understand the potential health effects, emergency medical personnel should understand the basic principles and terminology of toxicology.

Chemicals are often grouped according to their effect on the body, the classes being differentiated according to the primary organ system that is affected by exposure.

Typical classes are:

■ **nerve agents or gases** – sarin, soman, tabun and VX gas

■ **vesicants, blister or cutaneous agents** – mustard gas, lewisite

■ **lung gases, respiratory or choking agents** – chlorine, phosgene

■ **blood gases or systemic agents** – hydrogen cyanide, cyanogen

■ **irritants** – riot control agents, tear gas

■ **psychotropic agents** – LSD.

(See Resource IV, *Medical protocols for key chemical agents*, for the degree of clinical effects and recommended treatments.)

Characteristics of chemical agents

Toxic chemicals often produce injuries at the point where they come into contact with the body, typically the skin and the mucous membranes of the eyes, nose, mouth or respiratory tract. In addition, a toxic chemical may be absorbed into the bloodstream and distributed to other parts of the body, producing systemic effects. Generally, the effects of chemical agents will depend on the concentration level of the release, and the health and other factors determining the susceptibility to adverse affects of the individual exposed. Some of the effects may be delayed, sometimes as long as 48 hours or more. Health effects can be acute or chronic.

A chemical agent may be classified in a variety of ways. The most common form of classification is according to degree of effect of the agent – whether it is harassing, incapacitating or lethal.

Harassing agents disable exposed people for as long as they remain exposed. Sufferers are acutely aware of the discomfort caused by the agent, and usually remain capable of removing themselves from exposure to it unless they are prevented. Usually they will recover fully in a short time after exposure ends, with no medical treatment required.

Incapacitating agents also disable, but people exposed may not be aware of their predicament, or may be unable to move away from the exposed environment. The effect may be prolonged, but recovery may be possible without specialized medical aid.

Lethal agents, such as the nerve agent sarin, cause death of those exposed. The consequences of failing to detect a lethal but odourless, colourless, tasteless material are likely to be severe for those in the immediate vicinity of an attack and without immediate access to the appropriate PPE.

Respiratory agents, such as chlorine and the other respiratory irritants, exert their primary effect on the lungs, while the nerve agents and hydrogen cyanide are absorbed through the lungs and cause systemic effects.

Cutaneous agents: some (such as vesicants) primarily cause damage to the skin while others (such as nerve agents) can be absorbed across the skin and cause systemic effects.

A further characteristic refers to duration of the hazard. The word persistence refers to the length of time (in hours/days/months) an agent remains as a liquid causing infection or sickness. This length of time would depend on whether the duration of exposure is more than 24 hours per individual chemical. Persistent agents will remain in the area where they are applied for long periods (sometimes up to a few weeks). They are generally low-volatility substances that contaminate surfaces and present a primary danger in contact with the skin. A secondary danger is inhalation of vapours that may be released if ambient conditions allow. Persistent agents may consequently be used for creating obstacles, for contaminating strategic places or equipment, for area denial, or for causing casualties. Protective footwear and/or skin-protective clothing will often be required in contaminated areas, usually together with respiratory protection. Mustard gas is an example of a persistent chemical agent.

Non-persistent agents do not stay long in the area of application. They are volatile substances which evaporate or disperse rapidly, and may consequently be used to cause casualties in an area which needs to be occupied soon after the area has been cleared. Surfaces are generally not contaminated, and the primary danger is from inhalation, and secondarily from skin exposure. Respirators will be the main form of protection required. Protective clothing may not be necessary if concentrations are below skin toxicity levels. Hydrogen cyanide and phosgene are typical non-persistent agents, although phosgene can persist in low-lying areas for some time.

Table 7.1 Toxicity and persistency levels of chemical agents

Type	Agent	Physical state	Entrance	LT50	ICT50	Toxicity rate	Persistence Summer	Winter	Decontamination
Nerve	Tabun	Liquid	Eyes, lungs	400 R	300 R	Low	10 min-24 h	2hr-3 days	Soap and water
	Sarin	Liquid	Eyes, lungs	70-100 R	35-75 R	Low	2 days-several weeks	quick	Soap and water
	Soman	Liquid	Eyes, lungs	70 R	50-300 R	Low	10-60 minutes	slow	Soap and water
	VX	Liquid	Eyes, lungs	30-100 R	24-50 R	Low	2-7 days	2days to weeks	Soap and water
Blister	Mustard gases	Liquid >14.5°	Eyes, skin, lungs	1500 R	150 O	Cumulative	3-7 days	weeks	Soap and water
	Mustard gas	Liquid	Eyes, skin, lungs	1500 R	150 O	Cumulative	3-7 days	weeks	Soap and water
	Lewisite	Liquid >0°C	Eyes, skin, lungs	1200-1500 R	<300 O	Cumulative	1-3 days	weeks	Soap and water
	HL Mustard/ Lewisite mixture	Liquid		1500 R	200 O	Cumulative	<HD		
	Phosgene Oxime	Solid or liquid	Lungs	3200 R	>3 O	Cumulative	days	days	Water
Blood	Hydrogen cyanide	Vapour or liquid	Lungs	1000-4000R	Varied O	1-10 minutes	minutes		None required or none usually required
	Cyanogen chloride	Vapour liquid	Lungs	11000 R	7000 O	10-60 minutes	minutes		None required or none usually required

R, Respiratory (breathing); O, ocular (eyes).

HD = high density; LT50 = lethal toxicity (mg min-1 m-3), lethal exposure for 50% of population; ICT50 (mg min-1 m-3), incapacitation exposure for 50% of population.

Sources: adapted from www.trentu.ca/cemc, www.dera.gov.uk, www.preparedness-center.com.

Influencing factors

The risk of damage to health will be influenced by the type of agent, the amount, the method of dissemination, factors influencing its toxicity both during and after its release, its movement and dilution in the atmosphere, and the state of protection and susceptibility of those exposed. Toxic release will require toxicological advice from chemical and poisons specialists (see Resource IX, *Directory of organizations and conventions*).

Means of dissemination of chemical release

The dissemination of a chemical agent may be carried out mechanically by spraying, rupturing a container, using explosives, or by a thermal process. The major risk comes from their dispersal as aerosols or vapours.

Aerosols are finely divided liquid and/or solid substances suspended in the atmosphere. Sometimes dissolved gases are also present in the liquids in the aerosols. Aerosol clouds of a chemical agent can be generated by thermal munitions and aerosol spray devices, or as by-products of liquid spray devices and bursting munitions. Aerosol particles of a certain size accumulate over time in the respiratory system.

Dispersion – meteorological factors

The successful application of chemical weapons is difficult. It will depend greatly on climatic variables that are often difficult to predict, such as wind and rain.

Depending on the mechanism of deliberate release, there will be an area with a radius of 1 km in which the chemical agent will be dispersed as droplets. Droplet dispersion is the most serious threat.

As a vapour cloud is carried downwind, currents in the atmosphere cause it to spread both horizontally and vertically at a rate that depends strongly on the degree of atmospheric turbulence, resulting in lower dosages with large downwind and crosswind distances from the source. If the atmosphere is relatively stable, and depending on the nature and amount of the agent, dosages may reach hazardous levels even many kilometers downwind of the source.

- Some gases are rapidly fatal, but can quickly break down in the atmosphere.

- Higher air temperatures may cause the evaporation of aerosol particles.

- Light rain disperses a chemical agent.

- Heavy rain can dilute and disperse a chemical agent, driving it into the ground or washing away liquid agents (but can cause unintended contamination in other areas).

- Wind speed determines the pace at which a plume moves.

chapter seven

Routes of exposure

Routes of exposure may include:

- inhalation – affecting the respiratory system and breathing

- skin absorption

- ingestion (of contaminated food or water) can lead to chemical agents entering the digestive system – this is the easiest exposure to avoid if the contaminated sources are known.

Health effects of released chemicals

Chemical agents can cause acute systemic, critical or chronic health effects.

Vapours can be absorbed by the lungs only as long as the individual remains in the toxic atmosphere. Vapour from nerve agents, cyanide and phosgene do not penetrate the skin at concentrations likely to be present at the scene.

Clinical effects

Significant concentrations in the air may cause death, serious symptoms, mild symptoms or no symptoms at all, depending on the type of agent. Primary effects may be irritation, suffocation and chemical burns. The eyes are particularly sensitive to chemical agents and may develop symptoms of exposure very quickly and at relatively low concentrations, depending on the chemicals involved.

Liquid spills and aerosols

Many modern chemical warfare agents are designed to penetrate the skin, and this is promoted by high humidity. The onset of symptoms after skin exposure to a chemical agent is usually delayed compared with respiratory or oral routes of exposure.

Health effects of nerve agents

Nerve agents (sarin, soman, tabun) are chemicals that interfere with the functioning of the nervous system. The onset of symptoms is usually very rapid, occurring within seconds to minutes of exposure to vapours, and within half an hour of exposure to liquid agents. No matter what the route of exposure, the sequence of symptoms is the same.

Mild:

- runny nose

- tightness of the chest

- eye pain, dimness of vision and pinpointing of pupils

- difficulty in breathing, and cough.

Moderate:

- increased eye symptoms with blurred vision
- drooling at the mouth
- excessive sweating
- severe nasal congestion
- increased tightness of the chest and breathing difficulty
- nausea, vomiting, diarrhoea and cramps
- generalized weakness, twitching of large muscle groups
- headache, confusion and drowsiness.

Severe:

- involuntary passing of stools and urine (defecation)
- very copious secretions
- twitching, jerking, staggering and convulsions
- cessation of breathing, loss of consciousness, coma and death
- pupil size may range from normal to moderately reduced (in severe cases pupils will usually be constricted unless hypoxia has occurred).

[Source: CDC, www.cdc.gov]

Chemical hazards

Precautions and protection

If caught in a chemical incident in the hot zone, it would be important to know the essential precautions to take. The following points provide a useful guide:

- evacuate the contaminated area immediately – leave the contaminated zone uphill and upwind, avoiding moving through the agent cloud (go in the opposite direction to which the wind is blowing)
- try not to breathe in fumes
- avoid skin contact at all times
- if it is at hand, quickly put on PPE (face gas mask and protective equipment – paper masks offer little, if any, protection against chemical agents)
- never try to do mouth-to-mouth resuscitation on casualties
- seek cover in a closed area, preferably high up in a building
- do not return to the contaminated area until given the all clear.

Management of chemical casualties

Only trained first responders wearing full protective clothing (level A PPE) should enter a chemical incident scene (hot exclusion zone). Full PPE should include a mask with breathing apparatus and complete body protection. First responders should try to do a brief assessment and initial triage of casualties to ensure the most seriously injured are moved out of the contaminated zone first.

Table 7.2 is intended for those dealing with casualties to tick the appropriate boxes, calculate the totals and compare them with the total indicators to identify the likely chemical agent used in an incident.

Specialist activities of PPE-protected first emergency responders would involve:

■ decontamination

■ sampling and laboratory testing

■ clinical containment

■ special inter-agency arrangements for collection of longitudinal data.

Laboratory testing of chemical exposure specimens would require special devices and testing techniques. This level of laboratory analysis and training is unlikely to be feasible for most NGOs: regional and possibly international assistance may be needed. For example, CDC and WHO have access to Level D laboratories which have the highest level of containment for infectious agents.

Treatment regimens

Standardized treatment would comprise:

■ maintenance of vital functions

■ decontamination of skin

■ specific antidotes with required dose

■ general symptomatic treatment

■ other specific poisoning treatment.

Decontamination advice

Liquid or solid chemical agents on the skin should be removed within two minutes. If Fuller's earth is accessible, apply the powder with gloves and wipe off once the liquid is absorbed, then rinse the affected area. An alternative is to use soap and water with a soft brush, which should also be used for solid chemical agents. It is not possible or necessary to decontaminate vapour exposure, although depending on the chemical involved, clothing may continue to release vapours for some time. (See the section on individual decontamination procedures in Chapter 3.)

Table 7.2   Chemical agent indicator matrix

Indicator	Nerve agents	Blister agents	Cyanide	Respiratory agents	Riot control agents
Appearance					
Prostration (extreme exhaustion)	Yes	No	Yes	No	No
Twitching	Yes	No	Yes	No	No
Coma	Yes	No	Yes	No	No
Bleeding from mouth	Yes	No	Yes	No	No
Coughing	Yes	No	Yes	No	No
Sneezing	Yes	No	Yes	No	Yes
Vomiting	Yes	Yes	Yes	No	Yes
Fasciculation (muscle contractions)	Yes	No	No	No	No
Skin					
Cyanosis (skin blue or purple)	Yes	No	Yes	No	No
Grey area of dead skin	No	Yes	No	Yes	Yes
Pain, irritation	No	Yes	Yes	Yes	Yes
Clammy	Yes	No	Yes	No	No
Sweating, localized or generalized	Yes	No	No	No	No
Eyes					
Small pupils	Yes	No	No	No	No
Normal, large pupils	Yes	Yes	Yes	Yes	Yes
Involuntary closing	No	No	Yes	No	Yes
Tearing	Yes	No	Yes	Yes	Yes
Burning, irritation	No	Yes	Yes	Yes	Yes
Headache, pain around eye	Yes	No	No	No	No
Dim vision	Yes	No	No	No	No
Blurred vision	Yes	No	No	No	No
Burning pain in eyes	No	Yes	Yes	Yes	Yes
Redness	Yes	No	No	No	Yes
Respiratory					
Coughing	Yes	No	Yes	Yes	Yes
Runny nose	Yes	No	Yes	Yes	Yes
Tight chest (shortness of breath)	Yes	No	Yes	Yes	Yes
Burning, irritation in nose	No	Yes	Yes	Yes	Yes
Cardiovascular					
Slow heart rate	Yes	No	No	No	No
Fast heart rate	Yes	No	Yes	Yes	Yes
Digestive system					
Defecation	Yes	No	Yes	No	No
Nausea	Yes	Yes	Yes	No	Yes
Total indicators	**26**	**8**	**23**	**11**	**16**

Source: US National Center for Environmental Health (ATSDR) and WHO Public Information on Biological and Chemical Threats

Table 7.3 Chemical agents – overview

Agent	Transmission	Signs and symptoms	Treatment
Lung irritants: phosgene	Exposure Attacks lungs, filling them with fluid	Choking, respiratory failure Onset may be delayed	Remove to clean air Absolute rest Oxygen Hospitalization
Blood gases: hydrogen cyanide cyanogen chloride	Exposure Interferes with movement of oxygen from blood to tissues	*Acute:* breathlessness, headache, dizziness, drowsiness, respiratory failure, convulsions, coma, cardiac arrest *Chronic sequelae:* blindness, mental confusion	Decontamination Oxygen Hospitalization Sodium nitrate Sodium thiosulphate Supportive treatment
Vesicants (blister agents): mustard gas lewisite	Contact with skin, eyes and respiratory system	Nausea, vomiting, eye smarting, voice loss, difficulty breathing Extremely painful, slow-healing blisters	Removal from contamination Decontamination Supportive treatment – pain relief, oxygen, supportive care
Nerve gases: sarin VX	Inhalation, ingestion or through skin Interferes with nerve pathways between brain and voluntary muscles	Headache, nausea, excess salivation Dizziness, disorientation, coughing, diarrhoea, difficulty breathing Respiratory and heart failure, convulsions, coma	Treatment is complex and specific. Three antidotes are of use: atropine oximes diazepam Will also require supportive and intensive care
Disabling agents– Incapacitants: LSD, agent BZ	Ingestion, inhalation	'Off-the-rocker agents' Confusion, hallucinations through to psychosis	Detoxification Supervision until effects wear off, sedation by qualified medical staff if required
Harassing agents: adamsite, agent CN, agent CS	Inhalation, ingestion Contact with eyes	Coughing, vomiting, smarting eyes	Removal to air

Source: adapted from US National Center for Environmental Health and WHO Public Information on Biological and Chemical Threats.

Treatment of chemical casualties

On the onset of the symptoms of nerve gas (saliva, tears, blurry vision, breathing difficulties) and suspicion of attack (victims choking and fitting), medical advice should be sought immediately. There is a specific treatment for every agent. Antidotes for chemical agent poisoning should be administered only by competent medical personnel. (See also Resource IV, *Medical protocols for key chemical agents.*)

Scenarios and case studies

Created scenarios and reference to past events may be useful to an extent in understanding the possible health effects and impact of an incident. The sequence of essential emergency response functions and levels of PPE that would be required can provide guidance on where it might be 'safe' to provide medical and humanitarian assistance in the clear zone.

Chemical agent scenario I – chlorine tanker crash

An industrial chlorine tanker crashed into a government tower building near an urban internally displaced people's camp and NGO project areas in a low-income country. It was not immediately known if it was a deliberate crash or an accident.

Chemical hazard characteristics and effects

Chlorine is a non-persistent gas that can evaporate quickly. The immediate effect of a release would be a large and growing cloud of toxic greenish gas, which would constitute a downwind hazard over several kilometres.

Clinical effects

The onset of effects may be delayed, but it is important to note that chlorine gas is a primary respiratory irritant: it attacks the lungs and mucous membranes of the body, causing incapacitation and choking. In very severe cases it can cause asphyxiation; in less severe cases it can cause delayed pneumonia-like symptoms. Compressed liquid gas can cause cold burns to the skin and eyes.

Emergency response actions

Classed as a hazardous material incident, full PPE and breathing apparatus would be necessary to rescue victims, given that chlorine, particularly in its compressed liquid form, could have a severe incapacitating effect on rescuers as well as victims.

A hot zone would need to be defined to encompass the endangered population and those potentially affected by the plume of vapour. It would be necessary for first responders to locate upwind of the incident to assess the situation and the damage. It would also be advisable to observe the weather – wind direction and atmospheric conditions – with a view to assessing the plume direction for vapour cloud movement.

Organized evacuation of people in the close vicinity of the hazard would be useful. Advice should be given to residents to go in, stay in, tune in, find a safe room upstairs if possible, and to seal all windows and doors.

No decontamination of people in the hot or warm zones would be necessary due to the non-persistency of chlorine, although there could be a risk of contamination of the clothing of those immediately affected. Individuals should be advised appropriately.

chapter seven

Treatment would be to reduce exposure and support vital breathing functions. Expired air resuscitation should not be attempted when the face is contaminated unless an airway with rescuer protection is used.

(See Resource IV, *Medical protocols for key chemical agents*, Chlorine.)

Chemical agent scenario II – sarin agent attack

A no-warning attack occurs, directed at the civilian population at large. The incident involves deliberate release of sarin by a truck sprayer in a confined, congested urban market area near NGO beneficiary project sites.

Hazard dispersal
Cloud dispersal of the chemical agent can spread downwind. After several kilometres the threat would be reduced as the agent becomes diluted, downgraded and dispersed in the air.

Clinical effects
Aerosolized sarin is a highly toxic, lethal, non-persistent chemical warfare nerve agent which is hazardous on exposure by inhalation, ingestion and skin contact. Sarin attacks the nervous system, overstimulates muscles and glands, and the nervous system becomes blocked leading to respiratory paralysis. People who were in the vicinity of the release could develop symptoms within five minutes: breathing difficulties, chest tightness, vomiting, headache, runny nose, drooling, convulsions, bleeding from the nose and loss of consciousness. With no treatment, casualties will stop breathing within a few minutes.

Population response
Likely spontaneous evacuation from the affected area; possible mass anxiety among people.

Hot exclusion zone
Full PPE (level A) face mask, including self-contained breathing apparatus.

Immediate actions required by hazardous materials specialists in the hot zone:

- determine the perimeter and establish hazard control zones (hot, warm and cold zones)
- identify the agent and character of the cloud; chemical agent monitors would be needed to assist with risk assessment and indication of secondary devices
- stabilize the incident.

Population alert
Public announcements to people in the affected area to: 'go in, stay in and tune in'.

Decontamination (level A PPE essential)
Sarin in liquid form in contact with the skin takes longer to take effect, and would require decontamination. Sarin vapour may also require decontamination, as the vapour could condense on people's clothing and then off-gas (re-evaporate), creating a hazard for the responder and a secondary decontamination risk. Anyone exiting the contaminated area, including responders and bystanders, must be decontaminated.

Casualties would have be sorted initially within the area so that the most serious survivors could be rescued from the source of exposure first, and their contaminated clothing removed.

The whole body should be washed with soapy water and rinsed, not sprayed as this would spread the agent. Eyes should be flushed with water for at least 15 minutes.

Medical treatment
Medical treatment would be required for management of acute effects from exposure.

Public health and environmental effects
Bodies contaminated by sarin are not hazardous.

Contaminated air disperses after a period, and soil contamination degrades.

International assistance
If requested, international organizations such as OPCW are able to call on their member states to provide assistance with:

- detection and decontamination equipment

- assessment of the medical situation and needs, and of the local infrastructure capacity and capability

- arrangements for medical evacuation if required

- coordination of medical teams in the field.

Chemical agent case study – chemical attack on Kurdish Population, Halabja, north-east Iraq, 1988

Event history

The Iraqi regime air-bombarded rural townships and residential areas, and the largest civilian population ever exposed to chemical weapons, with three days of intensive random carpet bombing with a cocktail of chemical agents including mustard gas, sarin, tabun and hydrogen cyanide. The nerve agent VX and the biological toxin aflatoxin were also probably used. In addition to chemical weapons use, for which there is forensic evidence, the previous Iraqi regime may also have used weaponized (highly refined) biological and radiological agents during the attacks.

The chemical gases were delivered by 200–500 kg bombs, cluster bombs, aerial spray apparatus with 100 litre canisters and 90 metre air-to-ground rockets. An Iraqi artillery barrage had forced the residents of Halabja out of their homes to where they would be most vulnerable to the instantaneous effects of the poisonous gases. Some 250 population centres and 31 uninhabited strategic areas are known to have been attacked from April 1987 to August 1988.

Survivors reported seeing clouds of gas and people falling unconscious or convulsed, and birds and animals dying. Initial estimates suggest that as many as 250 000 people may have been exposed at some level.[1]

Chemical agent characteristics and clinical effects

Whole liquid or vapour mustard may not have had an effect for 4–6 hours. Mustard gas is a blister agent primarily designed to incapacitate and cause large-scale casualties. Only 20 per cent of the agent is likely to have been absorbed and would have been enhanced by heat and moisture on skin; 80 per cent would have probably evaporated. Mustard gas burns to the cornea would have caused blindness, skin cancers, pain and ulceration. Effects on the lungs would probably have caused recurrent infections, asthma, bronchitis and pulmonary fibrosis so severe that lung transplants would have been the only possible option for therapy.

Sarin is a nerve agent which can cause liquid contamination of the skin and penetrate deeper via wounds. It could have affected people's eyes, nose and chest, and also have caused severe neuro-psychiatric disorders, skeletal-muscle effects of paralysis, convulsions and coma.

Hydrogen cyanide is a rapid asphyxiate of the type used in Nazi gas chambers.

Environmental effects

- Water was contaminated and ground water and animals were affected.

- Contamination of ground, soil and vegetation would also have affected milk, rice and corn nut produce.

Morbidity and mortality

It is estimated that approximately 5000–7000 people died as immediate casualties of the attack (out of total population of 70 000–80 000). Some 30 000–40 000 people were reportedly injured, many severely. Among these, 12 000 people were chemically injured.

No internationally accepted institution has established how many people actually died in the aftermath or have died in the ensuing years, but a number of stillbirths, childhood malformations and deaths have been recorded. Many affected people still suffer long-term effects, including cancers, infertility, birth defects and neurological problems.

Required treatment and resources

Decontamination of mustard gas on people would have been required within two minutes. No antidote exists for this agent. Diagnostic equipment, advanced treatment and surgery to heal extensive mustard gas burns would have been needed. Iraq, a low-income country, and in particular the rural areas of Kurdish Iraq, had a lack of essential medical resources and infrastructure and certainly no antidotes or life-support equipment, cardiac drugs or analgesics, plastic surgery or transplants at that time.

Initial emergency response

In response to calls for international assistance from the General Secretary of the Patriotic Union of Kurdistan in March 1988, Médecins sans Frontières Belgium and Holland sent medical supplies and an assessment team comprising two Médecins sans Frontières doctors and a pharmacologist from the University of Gent's Laboratory of Toxicology to the towns of Halabja and Anab.

Follow-up activities included the provision of additional supplies and field visits, producing clinical toxicological reports, and a report suggesting that WHO and UNHCR provide assistance on the Iranian side, where some 60 000 refugees had crossed over.

Longer-term developments

- Some international organizations have set up Halabja funds for the victims and given donations of medicines, medical equipment and programme personnel.

- Numerous medical bodies and specialists continue to treat and study the long-term effects. A Halabja Post-Graduate Medical Institute in Iraqi Kurdistan has been established for treatment, research and environmental safety programmes relating to long-term effects of chemical and biological exposures.

CHAPTER 8

Key biological agents

Characteristics

The chief characteristic of biological agents is their ability to multiply in a person over time. Biological agents are commonly classified according to their type, the most important being fungi, bacteria and viruses.

Biological agents can also be characterized by their intrinsic features: their infectivity, virulence, lethality, pathogenicity, incubation period, mode of transmission and stability.

- **Virulence** is the relative severity of the disease caused by a microorganism.
- **Lethality** reflects the ability of an agent to cause death of an infected population.
- **Pathogenicity** reflects the capability of a microorganism to cause disease.

Mode of transmission

- Contagious diseases can be transmitted by direct contact between an infected and uninfected person. Certain types of infection, such as haemorrhagic fever viruses and plague, are transmissible from person to person.
- Airborne transmission can occur through coughing or sneezing.
- Vector-borne transmission can occur via biting insects.

Routes of exposure

The principal hazard would be from inhalation, and the hazard is greatest if the agent reaches the target population in the form of particles within a narrow size range. Most biological agents affect the lungs in some way even if the respiratory system is not a primary target organ. The body is most vulnerable to this route of exposure because of the susceptibility of mucous membranes to infection.

Incubation period

The incubation period is the time elapsing between exposure to an infective agent and the first appearance of the signs and symptoms of disease associated with the infection. This is affected by many variables, including initial dose, virulence, route of entry, rate of replication, and immunological status of the host.

Detection

Biological agent releases are less detectable than chemical agents until symptomatic disease outbreak occurs. Early detection and recognition would be through epidemiological surveillance, which requires vigilance for unusual patterns and clusters of disease, particular geographical features and characteristics.

(See Resource IX, *Directory of organizations and conventions, global outbreak alert and response network*.)

Specific disease indicators for an unusual disease outbreak

A weaponized biological agent outbreak will include unusual manifestations of disease, for example:

- pneumonia, flu-like illness or fever with atypical features (e.g. anthrax presenting as pneumonia)
- a single case of an unusual disease (e.g. smallpox)
- groups of individuals becoming ill around the same time
- sudden increase of illness in previously healthy individuals
- large number of clinical cases among exposed individuals within 48–72 hours of an attack
- unusually high prevalence of respiratory involvement
- more severe disease than expected for a given pathogen
- sudden increase in non-specific illnesses with –
  - bleeding disorders
  - unexplained rashes and mucosal or skin irritation, particularly in adults
  - neuromuscular illness such as muscle weakness and paralysis
  - diarrhoea
- illness type highly unusual for the geographic area
- casualty distribution aligned with wind direction
- rapid, large outbreak of similar disease in a discrete population
- many cases of unexplained death
- large number of ill or dead animals, often of different species.

Biodisease outbreak response

In a context of civil war, unrest and disease, it can be difficult to distinguish between natural occurrences of disease outbreaks and deliberate release. However, the immediate medical management and wider public health outbreak response would be the same, based on the principles of infection control, isolation and quarantine. This is a multi-disciplinary and complex task, requiring cooperation between the public health sector and medical personnel. Accurate reporting of clinical findings may be vital to alerting public health organizations. Once a biological agent is released it may not remain a local or regional event, but could become global.

Laboratory testing and diagnosis

The lead public health organization should investigate reported cases of a disease outbreak to confirm the situation. Clinical specimens should then be sent for testing. While local laboratories may have provisional capabilities for testing samples, specialized laboratory facilities and trained laboratory workers will often be required to examine weaponized biological agents and establish a definitive diagnosis.

The lead organization should set up an outbreak control team comprising relevant organizations: Ministry of Health, WHO, other UN organizations and NGOs in the fields of health, to:

- collect and analyse descriptive data (e.g. date of onset, location of cases)

- develop a hypothesis for pathogen source and transmission

- carry out sampling, screening and case definition and confirmation analysis (important but not essential in the first line response)

- make a differential diagnosis through professional testing methods

- follow up cases and contacts

- conduct further investigations.

Immediate protection measures

In the case of a highly infectious disease outbreak, protection measures would include wearing a filtering mask and goggles. Normal clothing of good quality affords reasonable protection against skin exposure. Skin contact with a biological agent – bacteria or fungi –should be treated immediately with soap and water decontamination.

The CDC classifies biological agents in two categories:

- category A agents would cause the gravest harm to the population at risk

- category B agents are more incapacitating and cause significant morbidity; less mortality.

Table 8.1 Health aspects of key biological agents

Agent	Transmission	Incubation period	Clinical syndrome, major symptoms	Infection control PPE*	Isolation	Treatment
Anthrax (Bacillus anthracis bacteria)	Airborne (inhalation)** Skin absorption	1-7 days (up to 8 weeks)	Flu-like symptoms, 2-4 days: fever, fatigue, chest discomfort followed by severe respiratory problems (black scar)	Pulmonary: None Cutaneous: Universal	Side room Side room	Antibiotics: Ciprofloxacin or Benzylpenicillin Vaccine (risk assessed on case-by-case basis)
Brucellosis or brucella (bacteria found in domestic animals)	Airborne (inhalation) Ingestion (swallowing) Absorption (skin abrasions)	5-60 days	Flu-like symptoms: fatigue, fever, depression, weight loss, swollen joints, abscesses of internal organs, genito-urinary, cardiovascular or neurological	Universal	Side room	Antibiotic treatment: Ciproxin + Rifampicin or Streptomycin Symptomatic, supportive treatment
Botulinum (toxin)	Airborne (inhalation) Ingestion Absorption (wound) Not contagious	1-5 days	Muscle weakness Skeletal muscle paralysis: symmetrical, descending Blurred vision, swallowing difficult, diarrhoea, vomiting, respiratory failure	None	None	Behring equine antitoxin Supportive treatment Intensive care
Ricin (toxin from beans of castor oil plant)	Ingestion Airborne (inhalation) Absorption (injection)	4-6 hours by ingestion 18-24 hours by inhalation	Irritation of mouth, throat, gullet, eyes, vomiting, bloody diarrhoea, fever, respiratory failure, lung oedema, abdominal pain, shock, massive bleeding	None	None	Supportive treatment Intensive care treatment may be necessary
Tularaemia (bacteria, six types)	Airborne release Inhalation, water, food soil contamination	Incubation 2-5 days Range 1-21 days	Pneumonia, skin ulcers, septicaemia, swollen lymph glands, inflamed eyes, general infection	Universal	Side room	Antibiotic treatment: Gentamicin or Streptomycin

	Transmission	Incubation	Symptoms	Barrier nursing	Negative pressure	Antibiotic treatment
Plague (bacteria)	Airborne or person-to-person Flea bites	1-4 days pneumonia 2-8 days bubonic and septicaemic	Severe pneumonia with quick evolution, swollen and painful lymph glands, can cause general intoxication (septicaemia)		Negative pressure	Antibiotic treatment with Gentamicin or Streptomycin Second choice: Ciprofloxacin
Q fever (bacteria in cattle or goats milk)	Inhalation Ingestion	10-40 days	Fever, systemic symptoms, liver and heart failure, pneumonia	Gloves	None	Antibiotics Supportive care (vaccine)
Smallpox (virus)	Person-to-person Infective droplets deposit		Fever, systemic toxicity; vesicular rash, ulcerating	Universal and masks	Specialist isolation hospital	Pre-exposure, post-exposure vaccine Supportive care
Viral encephalitis†		VEE, 2-6 days WEE/EEE, 7-14 days	VEE: fever, headache, malaise, photophobia, vomiting WEE/EEE: febrile delirium	Universal	None	Supportive care
Viral haemorrhagic fevers (virus)	All, including person-to-person	1-21 days	Fever, rash followed by general bleeding	Universal	None	Supportive care Ribavirin

*Universal precautions - gowns, gloves, eye protection and hand washing; barrier nursing - strict limitations on staff entering room, removal of gown, waterproof apron, latex gloves, eye protection in lobby and stringent hand washing before exit.

**Anthrax spores can survive for up to 70 years.

†VEE, Venezuelan equine encephalopathy ; WEE, Western equine encephalopathy; EEE, Eastern equine encephalopathy

All agents in Table 8.1 belong to category A, apart from brucellosis and ricin. (For further treatment details see Resource VI, *Medical protocols for key biological agents*.)

Infection control measures

Appropriate arrangements would be necessary, such as isolation or quarantine for contagious patients (airborne contact and droplets precautions). Assistance may be needed to:

■ identify a facility or create a separate temporary structure

■ mobilize medical equipment and supplies, and appropriate staffing

■ implement control measures specific for the disease

■ treat cases with recommended treatment.

Quarantine or isolation

■ observation of basic principles of containment

■ isolation methods – separation of the infection source/person from the unaffected population by preventing and controlling airborne contact and observing droplets precautions person-to-person during the initial stages of any unusual disease outbreak (e.g. Ebola, Marburg virus, smallpox, plague, SARS)

■ cutting routes of transmission by imposing strict limitations on freedom of movement

■ decontamination of clothes, supplies, linens and area (with disinfectant solution).

Medical treatment

Referral to an isolation centre would be required for all people with symptoms of:

■ mucous lesions (red spots, sores); persons with purple brownish discoloration

■ pneumonia with rapid evolution (fever); swollen, tender lymph glands

■ septicaemic patients.

Supportive care

Supportive treatment can decrease suffering and possibly save lives, but will depend on the availability of supplies of oxygen, bronchodilators (inhalers), and large stocks of antibiotics.

Treatment

A range of medical countermeasures can be used as post-exposure prophylaxis or as treatment for biowarfare agents, including vaccines, antibiotics, antiviral agents, and generic therapies designed to enhance the immune response system.

(See Resource VI, *Medical protocols for key biological agents*.)

Box 8.1   Resources for disease outbreak response

- Health personnel (trained staff only).

- Supplies (e.g. oral rehydration salts, intravenous fluids, water containers, water-purifying tablets, drinking cups, vaccines, monitoring forms, vaccination cards).

- Laboratory facilities (stocks of reagents).

- Communication links (between health centres, Ministry of Health, NGOs and UN).

- In an outbreak requiring an immunization campaign:

    - safe injection equipment (e.g. auto-destruct syringes and safety boxes)

    - transport (sources of emergency transport and fuel, cold chain)

    - immunization facilities (appropriate location and capacity)

    - cold-chain equipment (refrigerators, cold boxes, vaccine carriers, ice-packs)

[Source: WHO, 2003b.]

Health information system

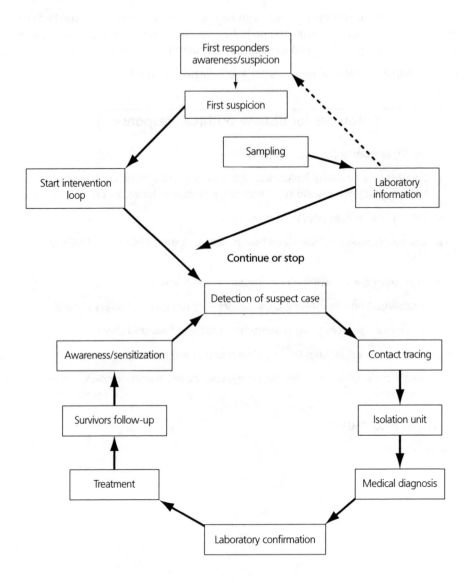

Figure 8.1 Response loop for biological agents. (Source: adapted from the Ebola Intervention Cycle.)

Scenarios and case studies

Bioterrorism scenario I – pneumonic plague

In a sub-Saharan African country, a person infected with pneumonic plague bacillus enters a refugee camp and intermingles with the camp residents throughout the rainy season.

Disease characteristics

Pneumonic plague can cause large-scale epidemics in humans. Plague is endemic in many countries in Africa, and over the past decade 76 per cent of the cases and 82 per cent of the deaths were reported from Africa.

Pneumonic plague is an infection of the lungs caused by the plague bacillus, and has a very high case–fatality ratio.

Incubation period (time from exposure to bacteria to the development of first symptoms) would be 1–6 days, most often 2–4 days.

Transmission

Droplets of saliva released by victims of pneumonic plague are infectious within a one metre radius. Pneumonic plague can spread from person to person. Inhaling bacteria suspended in droplets from coughing or sneezing by a person with pneumonic plague would transmit it. High temperatures, sunlight and dryness have a destructive effect, but rain would increase people's susceptibility.

Clinical effects

Among the camp inhabitants there would be a sudden appearance of symptoms: fever, cough, shortness of breath, chest pain, headache, weakness, sometimes bloody or watery sputum, 1–6 days after exposure, developing to severe pneumonia (lung infection). The pneumonia would progress rapidly for 2–4 days, and in 50 per cent of cases could lead to mortality.

Treatment

Antibiotics (e.g. streptomycin and gentamicin) must be given within 24 hours of first symptoms. Plague vaccines exist, but are not recommended for immediate protection in outbreak situations. Research is ongoing in the pursuit of a vaccine that protects against primary pneumonic plague.

Strict isolation and droplets precautions would be required. Chlorine would be an effective disinfectant.

Public health response

Once a case is suspected, local health authorities must be informed immediately.

[Source: adapted from WHO-EMRO 2003 and www.who.int/csr/disease/plague/impact/en/]

Bioterrorism scenario II – multiple aerosol release of anthrax

Incident
A large-scale aerial aerosolized release for several days of weapons-grade or fine-grade anthrax bacterial spores. The incident could go undetected at first, with numerous cases in the course of a week and initial deaths.

Characteristics
Infective agents can be disseminated as respirable particles by explosives or by sprayer. Large particles spread short distances – 100 kg could potentially wipe out a whole city. Anthrax is considered the highest risk bio-agent, but weaponizing to a low- or high-grade chemical is difficult.

Clinical effects

- Anthrax is an acute infectious disease caused by a spore-forming bacterium commonly found in the soil, which can remain dormant for years. Anthrax is not a contagious disease (it is not transmissible person-to-person), and inhalation anthrax is rare.

- Cutaneous anthrax could occur if a spore enters the skin through a cut or abrasion.

- The incubation period for inhalation anthrax is 1–7 days, but could be up to 56 days.

- Symptoms would be similar to a cold or influenza (fever, chills, dry cough, vomiting, chest or abdominal pains) for three days, leading to septicaemia, shock and sudden death. Up to 75–80 per cent of symptomatic cases can be fatal without treatment.

Treatment required

- Laboratory analysis of blood cultures (diagnosis could take up to 6 hours).

- Immediate dose of antibiotics (ciprofloxacin or doxycycline in three doses at 0, 3 and 6 weeks for up to 60 days, or 30 days if vaccinated). Penicillin if the strain is not resistant.

- Post-exposure prophylaxis after known exposure of people within the suspected area (reduces fatality rate by 50 per cent). Anthrax vaccine would provide full protection after three doses.

- Isolation not necessary.

Public health requirement

- Decontamination of individuals who came into direct physical contact/inhalation with biological spores.

- Removal and double-bagging of clothes.

Public health concerns

- Mass anxiety among the population.

- Overwhelming of hospitals and surgeries.

- Dead bodies could create a biohazard.

- Environment – long-term soil contamination.

- Decontamination of affected area, which could take years.

- Local produce inedible or at risk.

Bioterrorism case study – deliberate release of anthrax in the USA, 2001

Event history
At least four letters laced with spores of a highly virulent form of the anthrax bacterium (known as the Ames strain) were mailed to various prominent government and media offices in six locations in the USA. This led to a major bioterrorism investigation.

Disease characteristics
Inhalational anthrax – breathing of airborne anthrax spores into the lungs. Spores germinate into bacteria, multiply and secrete toxins that can produce swelling and tissue death.

Detection of the agent
Clinicians reported illness patterns or diagnostic clues that might indicate an unusual and infectious disease outbreak. Environmental and clinical samples were collected for laboratories to test for possible exposure. Direct contamination was found at the scene (post room), but residual contamination was negligible. Blood tests were taken to check for infections, although a person would need to inhale thousands of spores to develop an infection.

Treatment
Treatment was available but was not effective for half the inhalation cases (no treatment was available to destroy toxins). Inhalational and cutaneous anthrax were treated with a combination of intravenous antimicrobial medications. Five out of 11 patients with inhalation anthrax did not recover.

Areas for improvement
The main lessons learned were that more extensive coordination was needed among responders. There was an inadequate public health notification system to clinicians, and a need for better information management and communication with public health officials, the media and the public. The capacity of the public health workforce and clinical laboratories was strained by the incidents – they were unprepared regarding equipment, supplies and laboratory protocols to test for the volume of environmental samples. More clinical tools for response were required – vaccines, drugs and training of clinicians. The overall conclusion was that a strong public health infrastructure is required for bioterrorism emergencies in countries that have a potentially high threat level.

[Source: adapted from GAO, 2003.]

CHAPTER 9
Radiation and nuclear incidents

Access to functional nuclear weapons is unlikely, but suitcase-sized nuclear and radiological devices have in the past been reported missing from storage areas in the former Soviet Union. Such devices or conventional weapons could potentially be used as weapons of terror, to attack nuclear power plants, or radioactive waste-storage or processing facilities. Nuclear devices would be lethal; radiological devices are not always lethal if far enough away, but their psychological impact greatly outweighs their physical effects.

Hazard identification

Alpha, beta and gamma rays are odourless and colourless, and can be detected only with radiation detectors. Warning labels on storage containers can help with rapid recognition and identification of radioactive materials.

- Radioactive White I label – almost no radiation.

- Radioactive Yellow II label – low radiation levels, maximum 1 metre from the source.

- Radioactive Yellow III label – higher radiation levels, maximum 1 metre from the source.

- The number 7 at the bottom of the warning label is the UN hazard class for radioactive materials, and an indicator of a radiation hazard.

Figure 9.1 Placards associated with radiological incidents and materials.

Attack warning signal

In some countries a wailing (undulating) tone on sirens of 3–5 minutes duration, or short blasts on horns or other devices, repeated as necessary, would mean either an attack or a warning of fallout.

Radiation types

Exposure to radiation can affect the human body, and may come from a variety of sources. The four main types of radiation exposure are as follows.

■ Alpha particles – high energy, but cannot penetrate outer layers of skin, and can be shielded by a single sheet of paper. Danger arises from inhalation or ingestion of particles, which remain in the body causing continuing irradiation to surrounding tissues. These patients would not require decontamination, nor would they pose a risk to primary care staff.

■ Beta particles – high energy, typically found in fallout. They can penetrate the skin and cause burns, but the main risk is to the contaminated casualty who may ingest or inhale the particles, causing tissue damage. Aluminium foil or glass will stop beta particles.

■ Gamma radiation – electromagnetic energy waves are emitted like radio waves or X-rays, and will pass through the body causing cell damage. The distance from the source and the length of exposure would govern the effect. Concrete, lead or steel is needed to shield sources of gamma rays.

■ Neutron radiation – an ionizing particle with high penetration potential, requiring specialized shielding. This is released at detonation, but not found in fallout. Neutron radiation has extremely high contamination potential, 20 times more than gamma rays.

Nuclear explosion and effects

A nuclear explosion releases vast amounts of energy in three forms:

■ **Light** and **heat** – a blaze of light brighter than the Sun is produced, and the heat rays from an explosion can travel at the speed of light. Several seconds may pass after a person has seen the light or felt the heat before the blast wave reaches them, depending on the distance they are from the explosion. Heat and light waves can start fires some 15–20 miles away.

■ **Blast** – complete destruction of buildings at distances from the centre of explosion (depending on size of yield), and danger from flying glass, bricks and other debris

■ **Radiation** – immediate danger of exposure and residual radioactive fallout of particles.

General effects

While the destructive action of conventional explosions is due almost entirely to the transmission of energy in the form of a blast wave, with resulting mechanical damage, the energy of a nuclear explosion is transferred to the surrounding medium in the three forms listed above: thermal radiation, blast and nuclear radiation. The distribution of energy between these three forms will depend on the yield of the weapon, the location of the burst, and the characteristics of the environment. For a low-altitude atmospheric detonation of a moderate-sized weapon in the kiloton range, the energy is distributed roughly as follows:

- 50 per cent blast

- 35 per cent thermal radiation, made up of a wide range of the electromagnetic spectrum including infrared, visible and ultraviolet light, and some soft X-ray emitted at the time of the explosion; and

- 15 per cent nuclear radiation, made up of 5 per cent initial ionizing radiation consisting chiefly of neutrons and gamma rays emitted within the first minute after detonation, and about 10 per cent residual nuclear radiation (the hazard in fallout).

Local radioactive fallout effects

Thermal radiation will burn skin directly exposed to heat from the detonation.

The amount of energy released depends on the size and design of the device or facility. The effects would depend on whether the device was exploded high in the air, or on or near the ground. An air burst usually produces more fire and blast damage than a ground burst, which results in a crater and more radioactive fallout. Millions of tons of pulverized earth, stones, brick and other materials are drawn up into a fireball and become radioactive. Some of the heavier particles spill out around the point of explosion, and the remaining particles are sucked up into the mushroom cloud. Radioactive material is carried by winds and can settle in irregular patterns hundreds of miles from the explosion.

The primary hazard would be from dust contaminated with radioactive sources. The entire blast zone would be exposed to local fallout. The specific radioactive material, quantity, physical state, mode of release and prevailing wind patterns all contribute to the deleterious effects of a radioactive incident. It would start to deposit 10–15 minutes after detonation in the area around ground zero, and continue to deposit locally over the following 24–48 hours from a cloud, determined by wind and other meteorological and geographic factors. Radioactivity cannot be seen, felt or smelt, therefore respiratory protection would be needed to protect airways from the risk of radioactive dust. Contamination of the fallout zone might require relocation and decontamination.

- Actual ignition of materials exposed to thermal radiation is highly dependent on the width of the thermal pulse (which depends on weapon yield) and the nature of the material, particularly its thickness and moisture content.

- At locations close to ground zero, where the radiant thermal exposure exceeds 125 cm^2, almost all ignitable materials will flame, although burning may not be sustained.

- At greater distances only the most easily ignited materials will flame, although charring of exposed surfaces may occur.

- The probability of significant fires following a nuclear explosion depends on the density of ignition points, the availability and condition of combustible material (whether hot, dry, wet), wind, humidity and the character of the surrounding area.

- Incendiary effects are compounded by secondary fires started by the blast-wave effects, such as from upset stoves and furnaces, broken gas lines, etc. A fire storm burns in on itself with great ferocity and is characterized by gale-force winds blowing in towards the centre of the fire from all points of the compass (in Hiroshima a tremendous fire storm developed within 20 minutes of detonation).

Summary of effects

Blast, brilliant flash of light, high-energy radiation, extreme heat, mushroom cloud from radioactive material with fallout after 10–15 minutes and tens of miles downwind. The radioactivity in fallout weakens rapidly in the first hours after an explosion.

Clinical effects

Nuclear explosions in the air rather than on the ground are more likely to produce a greater number of serious burns through the heat flash.

Radiation illness develops slowly and has a cumulative effect on the body. In the survivors the main effects of damage from ionizing radiation result from DNA, cellular and organ damage, cancers, birth defects, infertility, immune system dysfunction, cataracts and nervous system damage (especially in the fetus and neonate).

Protection against radiation

A useful strategy would be:

- **Time** – decrease the amount of time spent near the source of radiation. Stay in the shelter until radiation has been measured and the all clear is given.

- **Distance** – increase distance from a radiation source. The strength of radiation is reduced the farther one is from the fallout.

- **Shielding** – increase the shielding between a person and the radiation light source. The most effective protection is to place some heavy material between the person and the fallout.

Precautions

Protective action should be taken – tune into the radio for instructions and advice. Being inside a building or a vehicle can provide shielding from some kinds of radiation. If outside when an explosion occurs, it is advisable to move immediately (within 10 minutes) away from the radioactive fallout cloud in a direction away from the blast centre, and observe the direction in which the wind is blowing the cloud. Protective cover and shelter should be sought. During an emergency involving radioactive materials, the safest place in a building is a centrally located room, the upper floors of a multistorey building (three storeys below the roof), or underground in a basement. This area should have as few windows as possible. If indoors during the blast, the best advice is to cover the nose and mouth, remain indoors, close windows and doors, shut down ventilation systems, and exit only when it is declared safe.

Detection by appropriate authorities

As radioactivity cannot always be detected by the senses, there are three ways to know that there is a risk of radiation.

- Fallout from a nuclear explosion can be visible as **dust**. The presence of dust is an immediate indicator of contamination.

- Authorities who monitor radioactivity with special instruments may give the alert, so ensure your NGO is connected to a **contact network**. If sirens or warning systems sound following a nuclear attack, the warning may mean another attack is approaching your area.

- After an explosion or radiation release, individual radioactivity dose can be measured with an electronic dosimeter device only if it has been used to measure the radioactivity level prior to the incident.

Authorities would be responsible for ascertaining:

- levels of exposure (radioactive fallout, doses of radiation, pollution of water, food, environment)

- exclusion zones (30 km), information zones (5 km) and resettlement zones

- means of protection – advice on shielding, sheltering in-place, and creating 'safe rooms'

- effects of exposure and symptoms – radiation illness: blindness, skin loss, mass burns, intoxication

- treatment – medication

- long-term health monitoring

■ assessment of water safety in the event of suspected radioactive contamination of water supplies, which would need to involve a radiation health specialist. The health effects of drinking water contaminated with radioactive materials present long-term health issues.

Individual contamination detection and monitoring

■ In the contamination-monitoring tent personnel must wear PPE with a respirator.

■ Practical decontamination of radiologically contaminated patients should be easily accomplished without interfering with required medical care.

■ Radioactive contamination of water supplies can be detected using standard radiation detection devices, but these require training for accurate reading.

■ Separate monitoring and decontamination stations (or tented extensions to a health facility) should be set up.

Evacuation following radiation exposure

Evacuation is advisable as soon as doses of irradiation increase. Return to contaminated areas should occur only after nuclear experts have given the all clear.

Factors related to the individual

■ Experience, personal loss, perception of threat, personal coping ability.

■ Normal reaction to abnormal events can lead to 'chronic environmental stress disorder'. The severity of psychological reactions would depend on factors related to the incident such as abruptness, intensity, duration, and availability of social support.

■ Stress reactions: early – nausea, muscle tremors, sweating, dizziness, chills, increased heart rate, blood pressure, hyperventilation; late – fatigue, drug use, sleeping difficulty.

Why people fear ionizing radiation

■ It is an unknown threat and cannot be seen or felt.

■ Fear of long-term consequences of radiation exposure.

■ There is a lack of education of the general public.

Management of psychological consequences after an incident/accident

Medical response, public health follow-up, community accountability, social assistance, government action guidelines, international guidance, education and counselling might be required.

Scenarios and case studies

Radiation scenario – a 'dirty bomb'

A truck or car explodes in a medium-density city in a country where NGOs are providing humanitarian assistance to population groups affected by a complex emergency. The incident involved the use of radiological dispersal devices with a highly active radiation material by means of a dirty bomb. There could be the possibility of multiple hazards and a secondary device. Further explosions occur, fire engulfs nearby vehicles and buildings.

Bystanders' response

There is likely to be widespread fear and panic in bystanders, spontaneous evacuation, relocation and mass anxiety.

Characteristics of radiological devices

A dirty bomb combines conventional explosives such as dynamite or semtex with radioactive materials around the explosive core. Given that radiation is invisible, odourless and tasteless, this would probably mask the discovery of a radiological attack.

Immediate effects

- The device would kill bystanders by blast and shrapnel. Possibly 20 per cent direct blast fatalities.

- Blast would burn skin directly exposed to heat.

- There would be risk of approximately 70 per cent minor injuries from the explosion, and of inhalation of radioactive material from dust and smoke in the air.

Secondary/longer-term effects

- Radiation exposure (although radiation effect would probably be low).

- There would be local fallout in the entire blast zone. Main fallout risk would be shortly after detonation around ground zero, and fallout could continue to emit for 1–2 days from a cloud containing radioactive materials, depending on wind and weather conditions.

- Birds would be observed falling from the sky.

- There may be fires and disruption of power, water, communications and other critical infrastructure. Local facilities in the vicinity may be unusable.

- Environmental effects – food would be inedible within the contaminated area; the air may contain radioactive materials during cloud passage.

Clinical effects

Symptoms would depend on the amount of radiation absorbed (radiation doses are measured in rem).

- First symptoms – nausea, vomiting, diarrhoea (several days).

- Secondary symptoms – fatigue, appetite loss, nausea, vomiting, diarrhoea, seizures, coma.

- Conventional explosive shrapnel wounds would present increased radiation exposure.

- Cutaneous radiation syndrome – skin redness, swelling, itching, hair loss (can take months or years to heal).

- Inhalation of radioactive materials is not a medical emergency, and there may not be any immediate fatalities as a result of a dirty bomb. Alpha emitters pose a danger only when inhaled (symptoms within hours) or ingested. It can take hours to accumulate enough radiation from a dirty bomb to cause radiation sickness or to develop cancer, and particles are easily shielded.

- Mass anxiety and psychosomatic symptoms are possible effects.

- Secondary hazard of residual contamination (elevated risk of cancer manifested years later).

- Long-term effects – depend on numerous variables.

Individual precautions

Within a short radius of the release location, if outside, people would need to cover their nose and mouth with a damp handkerchief, use dust masks if available, shield from the hazard and take shelter inside the nearest safe building as soon as possible, close and seal doors and windows, and turn off ventilation or air conditioning systems.

If indoors, people should stay inside unless advised to evacuate. Advice would be given to:

- avoid contact with possible radiation sources

- decontaminate the whole body (removing clothing could get rid of 80 per cent of the contamination, and skin should be rinsed with lots of water)

- avoid eating, drinking or smoking near contamination zones until they are determined safe

- await the all clear signal before exiting, and ventilate buildings.

Best practice emergency response actions

Cordons, exclusion zones, hot and warm zones (PPE level B or C)

Set up exclusion and restricted zones with a perimeter surrounding the site of the explosion (people within this zone would be relocated from the contaminated area in the medium or long term).

Safe distance for a bomb is generally 500 feet (approximately 150 metres). If a radiation-related weapon was used, a more extensive exclusion zone would need to be established around the weapon, and possible aerial and ground surveys conducted.

Risk management – hot and warm zones (PPE level A required)

Hazardous control measures would need to be implemented by trained HazMat personnel. First emergency responders might not be aware of the radiological nature of the explosive incident, nor have radiation detectors to identify whether a dirty bomb was used. Gross decontamination of victims of blast and radiation would need to be carried out.

Fatality management (PPE level A)

At the scene, radioactive levels would require appropriate shielding and appropriate PPE when handling contaminated bodies.

Casualty decontamination (PPE level C)

Once casualties were medically stabilized, skin decontamination would be needed – concentrating on open wounds first, washing with soap and tepid water (3–4 minutes), and rinsing (2–3 minutes). Hair decontamination should use mild shampoo if available. Clean water would also be required for eye irrigation.

Triage

- The immediate concern should be traumatic injuries and underlying medical conditions.

- Nausea and vomiting history would have to be explored.

- Radiation exposure and contamination would be of secondary concern, and radiation detection and monitoring devices would be used if available.

Treatment

- The priority would be patient stabilization, burns and trauma treatment, and supportive care.

- Vomiting within 1 hour – priority critical care should be given.

- Vomiting after less than 4 hours – immediate decontamination and assessment.

- Vomiting after 4 hours – re-evaluation would be required up to 24–72 hours.

- Potassium iodate tablets are effective only if a radio-isotope of iodine is used.

- Psychosocial care may be needed, along with medium-term monitoring of people affected by radioactive materials.

Communication to civilians within the vicinity of the incident
Civilians should be instructed to:

- stay in, and turn off ventilators and air conditioners

- tune in to a radio for emergency response procedures and for information about radiation levels and how to avoid exposure

- avoid taking public transport if evacuating, and clean own vehicles if used as ambulance transport.

Environmental concerns

- Ground water would be a possible concern and would need monitoring.

- Soil could be contaminated in the long term and would need removal.

[Sources: various internet sites including www.who.org]

Radiation case study: Chernobyl nuclear reactor accident, Ukraine, 1986

Event history

The Chernobyl Nuclear Power Complex, 230 km north of Kiev, Ukraine, 20 km south of the border with Belarus, consisted of four nuclear reactors. The surrounding woodland area had a low population density, but 3 km from the reactor a new city had 49 000 inhabitants. The old town of Chernobyl, 15 km to the south-east of the complex, had a population of between 115 000 and 135 000 people.

While one of the reactors was shut down for routine maintenance, a test was carried out to determine whether cooling of the core could continue to be ensured in the event of a loss of power. The test process lacked proper exchange of information and coordination between the teams in charge of the test, operation and safety of the nuclear reactor, resulting in inadequate safety precautions and alerts.

Two explosions destroyed the core of Unit 4 and the roof of the reactor building. This produced a shower of hot, highly radioactive debris and a plume of smoke, including fuel, core components and structural items with radioactive fission products, which rose 1 km into the air and exposed the destroyed core to the atmosphere. The heavier debris in the cloud plume was deposited close to the site, but lighter components, including fission products and all the gas inventory, were blown by the wind to the north-west of the plant. Fires started in the remains of the Unit 4 building, resulting in clouds of steam and dust, causing further fires in adjacent buildings and stores of fuel and inflammable materials. An intense graphite fire was also started, causing emission and dispersal of radionuclides and fission products high into the atmosphere, continuing for 20 days.

The total power of the explosion was estimated to be more than 100 times that of the atomic weapons used in World War II.

First emergency responders

Emergency responders included over 100 firefighters from the site, with additional reinforcements from the local fire station and recovery operation workers. The firefighters and emergency workers received the highest radiation exposures (external irradiation), resulting in 31 deaths. Very little national or international expertise existed on fighting graphite fires.

Emergency actions and evacuation

Some 5000 tons (4920 tonnes) of boron, dolomite, sand, clay and lead were dropped on the burning core by helicopter in an effort to extinguish the blaze and limit the release of radioactive particles.

No legitimate authority was able immediately to address the situation and provide answers to questions about exposure levels and water and food safety. Within weeks of the incident some 116 000 people evacuated and relocated from areas surrounding the reactor and most contaminated areas of Ukraine and Belarus. A 30 km dead zone was created around the site, in which no habitation is allowed.

Radiation/nuclear environmental effects

■ Vast territories (about 155 000 km^2) of Belarus, the Russian Federation and Ukraine were contaminated, and approximately 8 400 000 people were exposed to the radiation in these three countries.

■ Trace deposition of released radionuclides was measurable in all countries of the northern hemisphere. Caesium 137 is volatile and can stay in the environment for up to 30 years.

Clinical effects of exposure

■ Distribution of caesium in all organs and soft tissues: cells die or their function alters. Most cases had internal contamination concentrated in the thyroid. Intake of radionuclides through inhalation was relatively small. (Acute radiation sickness is caused by external irradiation, which is relatively uniform whole-body gamma irradiation and beta irradiation of extensive body surfaces.)

■ Severe multiple radiation burns on over 50 per cent of the body surface led to the deaths of 10 out of 28 cases, mainly due to sepsis. The death toll was about 40 people, of which 28 were due to direct exposure at the time, and 10 due to fatal cases of radiation-induced thyroid cancer. A further 209 on-site were treated for acute radiation poisoning. Nobody off-site suffered from acute radiation effects.

■ The risk of leukaemia has not been found to be elevated, even in the accident recovery operation workers or in children. In summary, there is no scientific evidence of any significant radiation-related health effects to most people exposed to the Chernobyl disaster.

Long-term effects
Nearly 404 000 people were resettled, but millions of people continue to live in an environment where continued residual exposure has created a range of clinical effects. There may be a legacy of cancers, bladder and kidney diseases, childhood malformations and genetic mutations, and psychosocial effects, but there is no scientific evidence to substantiate this.

The contaminated surface extends 1 000 000 km^2, and the environmental effects are likely to persist for hundreds of years.

Contributing factors

The following factors contributed to the increased rate and prevalence of thyroid cancer in children and adolescents living in the most contaminated areas, with 4000 cases in Belarus, 220 in the Ukraine and 62 in the Russian Federation:

- radioactive fallout and contamination in large areas of the three countries and beyond – many villages and towns were not evacuated, and sites were not maintained in quarantine

- late iodine prophylaxis

- significant psychological disorders, caused mainly by mental distress.

Response deficiencies

- Assessments suggest that the event happened due to a combination of design deficiencies and lack of compliance with established operational procedures.

- Lack of inter-regional harmonization of surveillance and response mechanisms.

- Mass decontamination units and emergent medical care were also lacking.

- Early communication of protective measures would have enabled the population to escape exposure to some radionuclides, such as iodine 131, which are known to cause thyroid cancer.

Later actions

- Safety review projects for each particular type of Soviet reactor.

- There are some 700 safety-related projects in former Eastern Bloc countries.

- Establishment of an international radioecology laboratory inside the exclusion zone.

- EMERCOM of Russia has set up a *Directory on Radiological Conditions and Radiation Exposure of the Population in the Areas of the Russian Federation affected by the Chernobyl Accident for 1991.*

- Post-Chernobyl Russian support programmes have set up activities aimed at improving the living conditions of and medical, psychological and social assistance to children and women in the radiation-affected regions of Russia.

[Sources: NucNet Chernobyl, www.world-nuclear.org; EMERCOM of Russia, 1998.]

CHAPTER 10
Explosive incidents

Enhanced high-yield, high-impact explosions are man-made technological disasters resulting from either accidental or deliberate use. Explosive incidents can be multi-hazard and can combine unconventional weapons and improvised explosive charges with highly destructive lethal materials. The current trend and increase of high-impact bombings deploying a suicidal element with high-yield explosives in middle- and low-income countries has had a severe impact on civilian populations, causing mass fatalities and injuries.

Types of explosive ordnance and incendiary devices used in violent conflicts

- **Air-burst weapons** (deployed in Lebanon).

- **Fuel air explosives** (used in Vietnam, the Gulf War and Afghanistan) and **thermobaric bombs** – detonation causes a high-pressure searing fireball followed by a massive blast and shock wave. People under the cloud are crushed to death. A second charge is used to detonate the vapour. Outside the cloud are blast waves with a vacuum pulling in loose objects (similar effect to a nuclear bomb). Causes burning and suffocation. Also used as a psychological warfare weapon.

- **High-power microwave** or **electromagnetic bombs** can fry communication links and damage water distribution systems and hospital technical equipment.

- **Pipe bomb** – time-delayed device (can be concealed in backpacks or vehicles).

- **Truck bomb** – deliberate arson and explosion incident.

- **Vehicle bomb** – an explosive charge in or underneath a vehicle which might explode when a door is opened or the ignition key is turned, or the device may have remote detonation. Another type of bomb may be constructed inside the vehicle.

- **Letter and parcel bombs** – threats may be aimed at a specific target, or used as a tactical means of harassment. Bombs may be designed with a device trigger when an unsuspecting victim opens the package.

Threat assessment and preparedness

A warning may be given by an anonymous caller or an identified group wanting to draw attention to a cause or create mass anxiety and disruption. Consider any known groups that might be active in the region.

A bomb incident plan would contain procedures that should be implemented when a bomb threat is received, or in the event of a bomb explosion.

Precautions for explosives

- If you see something suspicious, stop, don't go near it.
- Evacuate and notify or await bomb disposal units.
- Follow instructions given by emergency personnel, who will restrict scene access.
- Turn off cell phones, pagers and other electronic devices.

Immediate effects

Explosions produce rapid expansion of pressure and heat. Possible immediate effects include:

- incineration of people and materials
- loss of life and multiple explosion-related injuries (burns, blast)
- coping capacities severely strained
- traumatized population
- destruction and collapse of buildings and other structures
- disruption of transport and communication networks.

Emergency response

- Emergency response would probably involve rapid search and rescue, fire-fighting, detection, hazard containment, hazardous materials risk control, site assessment, and decontamination of powder or fluid spills.
- Emergency medical assistance would involve triage of victims, treatment of life-threatening injuries, mass casualty first aid and medical assistance, stabilization, possible hospital alert, and transportation to area hospitals.
- Relevant authorities would be concerned with crowd considerations, incident site perimeters and security zones, tactical response, securing access routes for rescue vehicles and ambulances, and coordinating evacuation.

- Bomb squad – role would be to diffuse or dismantle a bomb or incendiary device.

Outdoor evacuation distances

If civilians are instructed to evacuate, minimum distances are generally advised according to the type of device (see Box 10.1).

Box 10.1   Minimum distances

Firebomb or incendiary device	100 ft (30 m) radius around the contaminated area
Pipe bomb	850 ft (260 m) radius
Suspicious package in a vehicle	500 ft (150 m) radius
Postal explosive device in a building	850ft (260 m) radius, or two floors above and below the floor where the device is located
Portable explosive device	1850 ft (565 m)

Clinical effects and treatment requirements

- Initial (shrapnel), secondary (penetrating trauma), tertiary (blast fall) injuries, amputations, fragmentation wounds.

- First, second and third degree burns – immediate first aid includes:
  - if the person is on fire – **stop, drop and roll** to smother flames
  - remove all burned clothing – if clothing sticks to the skin, cut or tear around burned area
  - remove all jewelry, belts and tight clothing from over burned areas and from around the victim's neck – this is important as burned areas swell immediately.

- Blindness.

- Punctured eardrums.

- Breathing distress.

Scenarios and case studies

Explosive incident scenario I – an enhanced high-yield explosive incident

Event history (a no-warning event)

A stolen ambulance with concealed military-scale explosives, parked close to an urban reception centre for internally displaced people, is detonated.

In the town centre, a truck containing highly combustible fluid and an explosive charge causes another massive explosion. Several other explosions occur simultaneously nearby at locations where large numbers of people congregate.

Aftermath scene

- Loud bang and whooshing sound from a huge force of blast.

- Thick plume of smoke and massive cloud of vapour.

- Dead and injured people, torsos, body parts scattered over the area.

- Extensive damage to buildings, broken masonry, windows shattered, debris, vehicle fires and wreckage, large crater.

- Devastation, chaos, fear, panic, displacement and spontaneous mass evacuation.

Explosives effects

- Plastic explosives have a high rate of detonation and a high shatter effect.

- Secondary charge used to detonate the vapour of fuel created a high-pressure fireball.

Clinical effects

- Crush injuries, wounds, eye injuries, superficial injuries, burns, shock and confusion.

- Hot zone would require:
  - exclusion and security perimeters
  - identification, removal and disposal of explosive devices
  - fire-fighting standby
  - explosive ordnance disposal
  - search and rescue resources
  - structural engineers' advice.

- Cold zone mass casualty incident assistance would involve:
  - triage
  - emergency treatment and medical care
  - advanced life support
  - intravenous administration
  - transportation of civilian casualties.

Voluntary aid services

Assistance may be required with provision of emergency items for evacuees, including temporary shelter, food, clothing, blankets, medicines, generators, cooking and household equipment, kitchen sets, jerry cans and water purification equipment.

chapter ten

PART III
RESOURCES

RESOURCE 1
Detection and monitoring devices

Definitions

Detection	a signal indicating the presence of a potential hazard, but not necessarily the quantification of that hazard
Identification	determining the hazard by group and type
Monitoring	a quantitative indication of the magnitude of the hazard over a period
Deliberate or no-notice device	an incident warning of an attack has not been given, preventing pre-deployment of assets against a device

Detection

Rapid identification of an agent would require the deployment of frontline detection specialists and equipment for chemical and radiological hazards and bioterrorism.

Detection equipment would predict the extent of the hazard area, enabling accurate operational decisions to be made on, for example, the extent of a cordon or the requirement for evacuation.

Detection, characterization and identification of a chemical or biological agent or radiological, nuclear explosive event should be carried out only by appropriate specialist units accessed through national authorities, or a specialist response organization within an international or multilateral coordination system.

Separate detectors would be required for each of the functions of detection, identification and monitoring. A large variety of detection devices are available, ranging from simple colour-changing paper to sophisticated electronic contamination monitors. Most CBRNE detection equipment requires regular inspection and maintenance, and must have a skilled operator to ensure useful results. Potentially faulty equipment that does not adequately detect the presence of agents can endanger health and safety, because detection devices can give nuisance alarms of 'false positives' or 'false negatives' (not alarming, or failing to detect).

Chemical detectors

Suspicious chemical incidents would require the use of personal dosimeters, survey meters and contamination meters. Detectors collect a sample of air and attempt to separate and identify the chemical materials contained within it. An alarm signal is given when the target material is detected. However, rapid identification is not possible for every type of chemical agent, and detectors can detect only a limited number of substances. Detection equipment would not predict the extent of the hazard area, this would require monitoring equipment.

Radiological detection equipment

Specialized equipment and training are needed to detect and assess radiological contamination. A range of radiation detection devices exist, from Geiger counters to personal dosimeters, for use by appropriately trained personnel, to work in contaminated sites or with contaminated patients. Only qualified people should attempt to evaluate the levels indicated using a device.

Types of equipment – examples

Low-tech
Tetracore Bio Alert Test Strip Detector Papers contain a dye that becomes coloured when dissolved in the target chemical.

M-8 Chemical Agent Detector Paper provides the means to perform a quick identification of liquid nerve and blister agents. It changes colour, but can identify only some potential chemical contamination, and may not be effective in detecting solvents or agents absorbed into the soil, or present in low concentrations.

M-9 Chemical Agent Detector Paper is in the form of a roll which can be carried on a belt. It is used by ground forces, and is placed on personnel and equipment to identify the presence of liquid chemical agent aerosols. It contains a suspension of an agent-sensitive red indicator dye in a paper matrix. It will detect and turn pink, red, reddish brown and red-purple when exposed to liquid nerve agents and blister agents, but does not identify the specific agent. As soon as M-9 paper indicates the presence of a chemical agent(s), protective action must be taken to avoid being grossly contaminated. M-9 paper could be used inside a safe room or stuck into a window sill on the outside of a building as an indication of chemical exposure or of a possible all clear.

High-tech
A **Chemical Agent Monitor** is used by the military to monitor contamination of personnel or equipment by detecting agent vapour, and requires special training.

Detection equipment would generally not be stored on-site by NGOs, or accessible in time to mitigate the effects of some nerve agents. Training in the use and reading of equipment is absolutely essential, and without this knowledge and competence, detection of chemical or radiation hazards must not be attempted.

Observation and surveillance

Personnel in NGOs can detect the presence of chemical agents by closely observing their environment. For example, effects on animals (insects, birds, dogs) and humans can be immediate (within minutes or hours) depending on the agent used. If a release occurs, it is likely that within a short period groups of affected people will exhibit similar signs and symptoms.

The national or regional meteorological office can advise on weather conditions and wind direction for chemical incident clouds or plumes of gas.

Rapid detection of biological agents is difficult; the detection of biological disease outbreaks must be based on epidemiological surveillance. Release of a biological agent may not have an immediate impact due to the delay between exposure and the onset of illness. Incubation periods vary from disease to disease, normally days to weeks. The first indication is likely to be the unusual clustering of illness (e.g. people who were at the same location or event), an unusual age distribution for common disease, or a large number of cases with 'unusual' symptoms.

Chemical and radiation specialists

A range of expert organizations exist for further information on chemical and radiological substances. See Resource IX, *Directory of organizations and conventions.*

resource one

RESOURCE II

Personal protective equipment

Personal protective equipment (PPE) refers to the ensemble of respiratory equipment, garments and barrier materials used to protect rescuers and medical personnel from exposure while they perform essential response functions in environments contaminated by chemical, biological and radioactive hazards. The goal of civilian PPE is to prevent the transfer of hazardous material from the environment or casualties to rescue workers or medical personnel.

Key issues

In any CBRNE event, the civilian population is unlikely to have warning of an attack. This also applies to the emergency services, which might be called out to a scene but may not be equipped with PPE or have sufficient capacity and capability. Different levels of specialist clothing and equipment would be required by different types of emergency responders, who must be trained in donning (putting on) and doffing (taking off) procedures and the use, safe practice and maintenance of PPE.

Four levels of PPE

Level A (level 1) PPE for hot zone emergency responders

- Level A would be appropriate for fire brigades, for use in the highest threat environment for identification and containment of hazardous materials, toxic gases and chemical incidents. The hot zone therefore must be restricted only to specially trained and equipped firefighters and hazardous material specialists.

- Level A would consist of a fully encapsulated, vapour gas-tight, chemical-resistant suit with self-contained breathing apparatus (SCBA), inner/outer chemical-resistant gloves, and chemical-resistant safety boots for the highest available level of respiratory, skin and eye protection from solid, liquid and gaseous chemicals.

Level B (level 2) PPE for warm zone emergency responders and activities

■ Level B PPE should be used when the highest level of respiratory protection is needed, but a lesser degree of skin and eye protection is required. This type might be used by fire brigades where the type of chemical agent is known, or for rapid administration of life-saving countermeasures such as distribution of antidotes in a hazardous zone. It does not provide protection against chemical vapours or gases.

■ Level B PPE provides splash protection through use of chemical-resistant clothing, e.g. overalls and long-sleeved jacket, two-piece chemical splash suit, disposable chemical-resistant coveralls, and a full face piece with SCBA on the outside of the gas-tight suit. It will also have inner chemical-resistant gloves, chemical-resistant safety boots and a hard hat.

Level C (level 3) PPE for warm zone medical assistance when the site and its hazards have been completely characterized

■ Level C PPE is not acceptable for chemical emergency response, but should be worn when the type of airborne substance(s) are known, concentration is measured, criteria for using air-purifying respirators are met, and skin and eye exposures are unlikely. It provides the same degree of skin protection as level B, but a lower level of respiratory protection.

■ This level involves a full face piece with air-purifying canister-equipped respirator, which will draw air across filters by a battery-operated source. Chemical-resistant clothing will include chemical-resistant gloves and safety boots, a hard hat and a two-way radio communications system.

Level D (level 4) PPE for the warm/cold zone perimeter

■ This level might be used by an emergency response service, but is not suitable for chemical or other hazardous incidents where exposure is a risk.

■ Level D could be used for biological outbreak protection.

■ Level D is primarily a work uniform. It would consist of coveralls, safety boots/shoes, safety glasses or chemical splash goggles, face shield (3M mask) and nitrile gloves.

■ It would provide no respiratory protection and minimal skin protection.

Principles of respiratory protection

Personal protective equipment should be aimed at 100 per cent protection of body and face. Protective clothing must be worn with a mask, and must be sealed from the outside environment. The mask must be sized and fitted for the individual wearer and an appropriate filter must be used for the type of agent dispersed. Masks must protect the oral and nasal passages as well as the eyes. Masks are designed for those who are trained to operate in a contaminated environment, enter to perform a specific task and leave via a decontamination process. If the type of agent is unknown, full SCBA (level A) must be used by first emergency responders as a protective measure. In the warm and cold zones, gas masks with respirators (minimum level C) must be worn with protective suits as different agents are transmitted by different means.

Types and features of respirators

There are two categories of protective mask.

- **Self-contained breathing apparatus (SCBA) and lung-powered filter (LPF)** systems – the SCBA requires an air tank worn on the back, but will have only one hour's supply and is cumbersome (18 kg) to carry. Generally used by firefighters in the hot zone (level A).

- **Air-purifying respirator (APR)** – purifies ambient air by passing it through a filtering element before inhalation. The APR consists of a face piece worn over the mouth and nose with a filter element that filters ambient air before inhalation. Three basic types exist: (i) powered, (ii) chemical cartridge or canister, (iii) disposable.

  Powered APRs deliver filtered air under positive pressure, and provide the greatest degree of respiratory protection. The respirator face piece material should be resistant to the key chemicals.

  Cartridges and canisters are designed for specific materials at specific concentrations. To aid the user, manufacturers have colour-coded the cartridges and canisters to indicate the chemical or class of chemicals for which the device is effective. The face mask must also make an effective airtight seal with the face to keep out vapour; should be a comfortable but firm fit with rapid head movement; should allow undistorted vision and make provision for spectacles to be used inside the mask without misting the lenses; should not be used with a beard. A speech-enhancement device will reduce distortion and regulate volume – the mask should allow for a microphone or headset attachment to enable talking by telephone or radio. The canister, designed with a filter to remove harmful materials, is the most important feature. Canisters must be capable of dealing with the likely type of agent, and respirator canisters must be changed according to the expiry time on the instructions. A variety of chemical cartridges or canisters, which eliminate a range of chemicals, are available.

Disposable APRs are usually half masks which do not provide adequate eye protection. This type of APR depends on a filter which traps particulates. The use of a high-efficiency particulate air (HEPA) filter, or use in combination with a chemical cartridge, enhances disposable APRs.

Constraints and limitations of PPE

Personal protective equipment is used to manage a hazardous risk in a CBRNE incident. If individual aid organizations decide to provide assistance to civilians affected by such an event, they will need to determine their own requirement for PPE. The following points highlight some of the constraints and limitations of PPE.

- **Time-consuming** – donning and doffing should be carried out according to set procedure and in pairs. Valuable time and effort would be wasted putting on a suit and mask, rather than taking appropriate measures to quickly move away from the threat.

- **Heat stress** – PPE has severe limitations in terms of its physiological effects on the wearer, and its durability and flexibility. It can be used only for a limited length of time. Wearing PPE equipment has a debilitating effect and will severely limit the ability to evacuate from a contaminated area. It can also cause health and safety hazards such as heat exhaustion, dehydration and work stress. Masks with drinking devices are rare in the first responder market.

- **Impaired mobility** – full CBRNE gas-tight suits can cause reduced mobility and limited vision, and make communication difficult.

- **Training requirement** – purchasing PPE without effective training and maintenance would give staff a false sense of security. Incompetent use of PPE can result in a greater health risk. Proper use and maintenance of PPE requires several days' intensive training to reach the minimum standard skill level, and must be continually refreshed, at least on an annual basis.

- **Physical constraints** – additional factors reducing effectiveness include facial hair, beards, age of the mask, variations in conditions during use, and the time since last practice of donning the equipment.

- **Decontamination requirement** – it is also necessary to decontaminate or discard PPE after exiting from a hazard area.

- **Psychological effect** – not least is the ethical issue and psychological effect of responders having access to and use of PPE when national staff and the civilian population have no protection against contamination.

Self-supporting breathing apparatus must be worn if the substance is unknown. Almost all technical disasters, including deliberate releases, have occurred without warning. Personal protective equipment provides protection only if used at a specific time, that is, within minutes of a release. So a mask and respirator would need to be with the user at all times – at work, in the vehicle, by the bed – to be effective. It is highly doubtful that NGO staff would have PPE immediately to hand at the onset of an incident and would be able to use it within the short time required. Personal protective equipment therefore might be best used for hazard avoidance and escape to the clear zone where humanitarian action can be taken.

Hazard avoidance and evacuation kits

A fitted protective mask combined with an overgarment, gloves and boots should provide sufficient protection for hazard avoidance and evacuation. Gauze masks serve as good protection only for secondary infection by biological diseases, and are not sufficient to protect workers at the source of an outbreak or release. Barrier nursing-level masks are likely to be more suitable for infectious diseases.

Boxes II.1–4 give suggestions of kits for rucksacks or vehicles.

Box II.1   CBRNE escape pack for field staff (belt pack)

Belt pack ☐

Gloves, butyl (nitrile or neoprene), inner gloves (latex) ☐

Nuclear, biological or chemical (NBC)-escape hood, smoke-escape hood ☐

Tyvek coveralls (white) for clothing change ☐

Tyvek QC coveralls ☐

Latex overshoes ☐

Bar soap, sponge ☐

Dustbin bags (2) ☐

Water-purification tablets, water bottle ☐

Duct tape ☐

resource two

Box II.2 CBRNE escape pack for field staff (rucksack)

Rucksack or backpack ☐

Tyvek F chemical-resistant coveralls ☐

Gloves (butyl, nitrile or neoprene), inner latex gloves ☐

NBC-escape hood; smoke-escape hood ☐

Air-purifying respirator, respirator cartridges ☐

Tyvek coveralls (white) for clothing change ☐

Vinyl galoshes ☐

Bar soap, sponge, dustbin bags ☐

Water-purification tablets, canteen, duct tape ☐

Insect repellent (permethrin for clothing, DEET for skin) ☐

Eye wash (4 oz bottle) ☐

Box II.3 CBRNE escape pack for field staff (day sack)

Firefighter's field pack with shoulder strap ☐

Tyvek F chemical-resistant coveralls ☐

Outer gloves (butyl, nitrile or neoprene) ☐

Inner gloves (latex) ☐

NBC-escape hood, smoke escape hood ☐

Air-purifying respirator, respirator cartridges ☐

Tyvek coveralls (white) for change of clothing ☐

Vinyl galoshes ☐

Insect repellent (permethrin for clothing, DEET for skin) ☐

Rubbish bags, duct tape ☐

Eye wash (4 oz bottle), water-purification tablets, canteen ☐

Box II.4 Level C PPE ensemble for medics/paramedics/WatSan

Tychem F or Tyvek F disposable gas-tight suit MKV (Du Pont) ☐

Air-purifying respirator and cartridges ☐

Tychem protective coveralls ☐

Chlorobutyl rubber gloves ☐

Chemical-resistant boots ☐

Medical countermeasures

Protective health measures

Prophylaxis

Deliberate use of biological agents has historically been low. The probability of covert use of biowarfare diseases may also be low, but the severe consequences of a deliberate release of a biological agent makes preparedness an important component of public health. The World Health Organization (WHO) recommends strengthening the existing infrastructure, reaching to the local level, rather than establishing a specialized unit for responding to a biological attack in a low-income country. Frontline responders involved in the initial management of biological casualties would need training in barrier nursing techniques, safe handling of samples and decontamination procedures, and should also have first call on personal protective equipment (PPE) and vaccines. WHO recommends that only key personnel likely to come into contact with smallpox-infected patients should be vaccinated prior to exposure; in some situations only selected laboratory workers, military personnel and primary smallpox outbreak responders may receive the vaccine. Therefore, pre-vaccination against potential biowarfare agents (e.g. anthrax, tularaemia, smallpox and plague) should not be prescribed, unless recommended by WHO, the US Centers for Disease Control and Prevention (CDC) or another competent health advisory body in the event of a large-scale outbreak. A global system of surveillance and response in real time would facilitate a rapid and rational call-out response for the necessary laboratory and epidemiological skills in those countries that lack the facilities to contain a disease outbreak.

Post-exposure vaccines

Although only smallpox and anthrax post-exposure vaccines prove reliable, with high degrees of protection against infection, they can have serious and sometimes fatal side effects. Vaccines currently available may not be protective when the exposure is unusual and characteristic of a biowarfare event. For example, the anthrax vaccine may not protect against inhalation of weaponized (highly refined) anthrax. Once identified, anthrax and many other biowarfare agents have a low mortality rate when properly treated.

Smallpox vaccine – limitations

- According to CDC, just one confirmed case of smallpox anywhere in the world would be considered a global emergency. However, the smallpox vaccine has a high incidence of adverse reactions and side effects. Therefore, widespread immunization would not be recommended in the absence of confirmed cases, and preventive smallpox vaccination is not considered an operational requirement for first emergency responders.

- Personnel vaccinated against smallpox prior to 1989 are not guaranteed immunity.[2] Previous immunity decreases after five years, and people again become susceptible to infection with smallpox.

- The smallpox vaccine is best used as a post-exposure therapy in the event of a smallpox outbreak. The side effects of the post-exposure vaccine are much less than the risk and complications of infection with the smallpox disease.

- One-time inoculation for smallpox (for post-exposure risk) should provide rapid protection against infection within seven days of exposure, but post-exposure vaccine would have to be used within a four–day window (and would need pre-planning, including an adequate on-site cold chain).

- Limited vaccine availability and cold-chain requirements in middle- and low-income countries could constrain post-exposure vaccination capacity.

Anthrax vaccine limitations

- The anthrax vaccine is not licensed or commercially available. The anthrax vaccine presently available is not recommended by either CDC or WHO for general use, nor for first responders or hospital personnel. The anthrax vaccine requires four doses over a period of seven months before providing adequate levels of protection, and therefore is not viable as emergency treatment.[3]

- Health Departments and Medical Coordinators of NGOs in medium- and high-risk countries are advised to consult key health authorities (WHO, CDC) to determine when and how these recommendations change.

  [Sources: www.cdc.gov and www.who.int/inf]

Other bio-agents

- Other biowarfare agents have a low mortality rate once the disease and symptoms are identified and treatment given, for example, pneumonic plague, brucellosis, glanders, melioidosis, Q fever and typhus fever.

- There is some empirical evidence that the use of antibiotics as post-exposure prevention against biological agents could be effective. Biological diseases can be treated effectively with a readily available broad spectrum of antibiotics as post-exposure prophylaxis with minimal side effects. Doxycycline and tetracycline are inexpensive and widely available antibiotics.

Stockpiling of CBRNE countermeasures

Inappropriate use of most CBRNE medicines and antidote kits can cause significant health hazards. They should be used only under the supervision of trained medical professionals at designated emergency response facilities.[4]

Stockpiling limitations

■ Antidote stockpiles would require sophisticated selection, procurement, secure storage and rapid distribution means.

■ Based on a threat/risk assessment of a specific chemical or biological agent, it would be necessary to ascertain prepositioning of specific kits at close range, location, content, quantity, shelf-life, permission for release and transportation with cold-chain facilities.

■ There are no regions where stockpiling of biological or chemical agent antidote or pharmaceuticals is recommended. Spending large sums can be justified only when there is consensus within a country that the threat is probable and specific.

■ WHO and CDC advise that there is no justification for using antibiotics as a preventive measure, therefore stockpiling beyond standard emergency preparedness is not encouraged.

■ Emergency medical kits of NGOs are not equipped for mass biological or chemical events.

■ Essentially, stockpiling of biological or chemical agent drugs or antidotes (including auto-injectors for nerve agents) is not recommended by the WHO or CDC.

Medical pooling mechanisms

■ Planners in NGOs should investigate all possible methods of timely procurement of appropriate medicines within the region, and coordinate with the proper local health authorities to assess risk and ensure availability.

■ If necessary, treatment would begin with in-stock supply and resupply would take place through the medical pipeline.

■ WHO has rapid procurement capability for medical supplies and drugs (see Resource IX, *Directory of organizations and conventions*).

■ The WHO Emergency Health Kit contains drugs and medical supplies for 10 000 people for three months. The full kit content list can be found on the WHO website: www.who.int/disasters.

Medical protocols for key chemical agents

Chlorine

Key characteristics

- Chlorine is a greenish-yellowish gas.
- It has an odour which is familiar from household bleach and swimming pools.
- Exposure can result from occupational and domestic use.

Effects, including signs and symptoms

- Chlorine is an irritant to the respiratory tract and mucous membrane. It may cause coughing, choking, reduction of oxygen to below physiological levels, and pulmonary fluid accumulation. In high concentrations it can be fatal. It is corrosive to the eyes and skin.
- Contact with compressed liquid gas may cause frostbite or burns to skin and eyes. Severe exposure may cause laryngospasm (closure of the larynx), airway obstruction, respiratory arrest and cardiovascular (heart) collapse.

Protection and decontamination

- Rescuers should avoid risking themselves, and wear appropriate full peronal protection equipment (PPE) and breathing apparatus (if available).

First aid

- Reduce exposure and support vital breathing functions.
- The casualty should be moved to a non-contaminated area.
- If the casualty is unconscious a clear air pathway should be established and maintained; give 100 per cent oxygen if available.

resource four

Case management

Inhalation exposure

- Patients should be kept at rest and assessed for respiratory difficulties using baseline lung function tests as appropriate.

- Give oxygen for patients with difficulty breathing.

- Give bronchodilators (e.g. salbutamol, orally or inhaled) for bronchospasm.

- Corticosteroids may prevent inflammatory response and early use should be considered in severe cases.

- If the patient stops breathing, expired air resuscitation should be carried out immediately using a pocket mask with a one-way valve if available.

- Expired air resuscitation should not be attempted when the face is contaminated unless an airway with rescuer protection is used.

Dermal exposure

- If frostbite occurs, do not remove clothing. Flush skin with water.

- If frostbite is not present, remove contaminated clothing, if possible under a shower of soapy water, and place clothing in double, sealed, clear (labelled) bags and store in a secure area away from patients and staff.

- Wash skin thoroughly with plenty of soapy water.

Eye exposure

- If the eye tissue is frozen, seek medical advice as soon as possible.

- If eye exposure is not frozen, rinse thoroughly with water or saline for 15 minutes.

- Refer to eye specialist if there is any uptake of stain (spot or discoloration of the eye).

Blood management

There is currently no analysis available to measure the chlorine concentration in blood.

[Source: adapted from HPA, 2003.]

Hydrogen cyanide (HCN) and cyanide salts

Key characteristics

- Cyanide salts are toxic, except for metal cyanide which rarely produces cyanide poisoning.

- Exposure to hydrogen cyanide may be fatal within minutes.

- Hydrogen cyanide is a colourless gas with a faint, almond-like odour. Sodium cyanide and potassium are both white solids with a bitter, almond-like odour in damp air.

- Cyanide gas is highly flammable. It is absorbed by inhalation, ingestion and through the eyes and intact skin. It acts extremely quickly once absorbed.

Effects, including signs and symptoms

- Clinical effects appear within seconds or minutes after ingestion or inhalation of a large concentration.

- In massive cyanide poisonings, other mechanisms may contribute to clinical effects such as pulmonary and coronary arterial vasoconstriction, causing heart pump failure and decreasing cardiac output.

- Eye effects such as eye infection and eyelid oedema (swelling) have been reported following exposure to irritant cyanogen chloride.

- Systemic toxicity could arise from optical exposure.

- Transient blindness has occasionally been reported from exposure to sublethal cyanide doses.

- Blindness is possible with cyanide-induced damage to optic nerves and retina.

- Key symptoms include giddiness, headache, anxiety, confusion, nausea and difficulty in breathing, rapidly followed by coma, convulsions, bradycardia, hypotension (abnormally low or falling blood pressure), metabolic acidosis (synthesis of acid in the body) and death. Loss of vision and hearing may occur.

- Most cases of acute poisoning will die or recover, but rare cases of long-term sequela have been reported, e.g. development of Parkinson's syndrome, memory deficit, personality changes or extrapyramidal syndrome.

Protection and decontamination

- In the event of a large spillage, stay upwind and out of low areas. Ventilate closed spaces.

- Rescuers must not enter a contaminated area without full PPE and self-contained breathing apparatus.

resource four

■ Casualties should be transported in a way such that there is no risk to drivers of emergency vehicles being contaminated by fumes. Remove casualties from the source of exposure, then remove contaminated clothing, keep warm and use soapy water for decontamination.

First aid

■ Terminate exposure and support vital functions. Move the casualty to an uncontaminated area.

■ If a casualty is unconscious, a clear airway should be established and maintained; give 100 per cent oxygen if available.

■ If the patient stops breathing, use expired air resuscitation immediately using a pocket mask with a one-way valve, if available.

■ Where the face is contaminated, expired air resuscitation is not used or attempted unless an airway with rescuer protection is used.

■ For dermal and eye exposure, repeat the above procedure.

Case management

Medical antidotes include cobalt, in the form of cobalt complex or as hydroxycobalamin, and sodium acetate.

[Source: adapted from HPA, 2003.]

Phosgene

Key characteristics

- Phosgene is a colourless gas and has a suffocating smell, like musty hay.

- It can be fatal on inhalation.

- Phosgene as a gas is likely to be ingested.

Effects, including signs and symptoms

- Exposure may lead to severe pulmonary, eye and dermal irritation which may cause frostbite burns.

- Inhalation: signs of toxicity may be delayed for 24 to 72 hours.

- Eyes: phosgene gas can cause smarting, irritation, discharge, swelling and pain. Liquid phosgene results in severe irritation, visual intolerance to light, corneal opacification and perforation.

- Skin contact with liquid phosgene may cause frostbite.

- Chronic clinical effects such as bronchitis and accumulation of air in tissues or organs can occur.

Protection and decontamination

- Decontamination, first aid and treatment must be performed only by rescue and medical personnel trained and wearing appropriate PPE with breathing apparatus.

- Remove casualties from the contaminated area or isolate them from surrounding contamination by supplying properly fitting masks.

- If no frostbite has occurred, remove contaminated clothing, if possible under a shower of soapy water, and place clothing in double, sealed, clear (labelled) bags; store in a secure area away from patients and staff.

First aid

- Terminate exposure by moving the casualty to a non-contaminated area and support vital functions.

- If the casualty is unconscious, a clear airway should be established and maintained; give 100 per cent oxygen if available.

- If the patient stops breathing, expired air resuscitation should be started immediately using a pocket mask with a one-way valve, if available. Where the face is contaminated, expired air resuscitation should not be attempted unless an airway with rescuer protection is used.

resource four

Case management

Inhalation exposure

- Symptomatic and supportive care is required. The patient should undertake no exercise and rest strictly in bed as soon as possible.

- Replace fluid to maintain blood volume; closely monitor pulmonary wedge pressure to avoid fluid overload.

- Patients with cyanosis (a bluish discoloration of skin and mucus membrane due to excessive concentration of reduced haemoglobin in the blood) require additional oxygen via a face mask or, if severe, an endotracheal tube. Consider early incubation of symptomatic patients using continuous positive airway pressure (CPAP) or positive end-expiratory pressure (PEEP) ventilation to reduce surfactant loss.

- Monitor blood gases, correct a metabolic acidosis (if present) with bicarbonate to 7.2 (slight acidosis aids oxygen delivery).

- Theophylline may be used for bronchospasm (may also alleviate bradycardia and hypotension). Administer antibiotics if indicated.

- Early administration of corticosteroids (e.g. methylprednisolone, 1 g per day for 5 days) may be considered to prevent pulmonary oedema.

- Take a baseline chest X-ray on admission, repeat at three and eight hours post-exposure, then according to symptoms.

Dermal exposure

- If frostbite occurs, do not remove clothing. Flush skin with soapy water.

- Wash skin thoroughly with plenty of soapy water.

- If eye tissue is not frozen, wash thoroughly with water or saline for 15 minutes.

[Sources: adapted from Department of Health, UK, 2001; HPA, 2003.]

Sarin

Key characteristics

A chemical warfare nerve agent, colourless in its pure form. It has a rapid onset of action.

Effects, including signs and symptoms

- Muscarinic (parasympathetic) effects – bradycardia (slow heartbeat or slow pulse rate), bronchorrhoea (excess discharge of mucus from the bronchi), sweating, salivation, lacrimation, vomiting, diarrhoea and constricted paralysis of the pupils may occur (subsequent blurred vision can persist for several months).

- Nicotinic (sympathetic and motor) effects – tachycardia, hypertension, muscle fasciculation (formation of small involuntary muscular contractions visible under the skin) and cramps, weakness and respiratory paralysis.

- Central effects: depression of central nervous system, agitation, confusion, psychosis, delirium, coma and convulsions may occur; effects on the central nervous system may be slowly reversible, or irreversible. Death is usually due to respiratory insufficiency and paralysis.

Protection and decontamination

- In the event of a large spillage, stay upwind and out of low areas. Ventilate closed spaces.

- Rescuers and medical personnel must not enter a contaminated area without full PPE and self-contained breathing apparatus.

- Sarin vapours may evaporate from heavily contaminated casualties and may pose a risk of emergency personnel becoming contaminated.

- Casualties should be transported in a way such that there is no risk to drivers of emergency vehicles becoming contaminated by fumes.

- Remove the casualty's contaminated clothing, place in double, sealed, clear (labelled) plastic bags and store in a secure area away from patients and staff. Place casualty in clean clothes or gown.

First aid

- Terminate exposure and support vital functions.

- The casualty should be moved to an uncontaminated area.

- If the casualty is unconscious, a clear airway should be established and maintained; give 100 per cent oxygen if available; excess secretion may require suction.

Case management

Inhalation exposure

If the patient stops breathing, expired air resuscitation should be started immediately using a pocket mask with a one-way valve, if available. Where the face is contaminated, expired air resuscitation should not be attempted unless an airway with rescuer protection is used.

Liquid exposure

■ Wash all skin parts three times with plenty of soapy water.

■ For eye exposure, irrigate thoroughly with water or saline for 15 minutes.

Drug protocol

■ Contact the national poison information service for further guidance and for paediatric doses.

■ Diazepam may have an overall benefit, as well as controlling twitching and convulsions.

■ Atropine hypoxia (reduction of oxygen supply to a tissue below physiological level) must be corrected before atropine is given: adult, 2 mg repeatedly, subcutaneously or intravenously until atropinization is characterized by decreased bronchial secretions, heart rate >100 bpm, dry mouth, dilated pupils.

■ Pralidoxime should be given as an adjunct to atropine, not as a replacement for it, and should be given in every case where atropine is deemed necessary. Traditional dose: 1 g (or 2 g in very severe cases) by slow intravenous injection over 5–10 minutes. 1–2 g 4–hourly (maximum dose 12 g in 24 hours) until clinical and analytical recovery is achieved and maintained.

[Sources: HPA, 2003; AFCOA Briefing on Chemical Weapons, cited in OPCW website.]

Mustard gas

Key characteristics

- Mustard gas is a vesicant chemical warfare agent, and is a powerful irritant.

- It has an odour of mustard, onions or garlic, but the odour can be detected only at concentrations that are close to toxic levels.

- Mustard gas can be in vapour or liquid form.

- Routes of exposure include inhalation and contact through skin and eyes.

- Off-gassing (re-evaporation) from casualties may be sufficient to cause symptoms.

Effects, including signs and symptoms

- In vapour or liquid, it causes damage to skin, eyes and respiratory system.

- Mustard gas does not cause pain at the time of exposure, and symptoms may be delayed for 4–8 hours. The higher the concentration, the shorter the time for symptoms to develop.

- Symptoms after 4–8 hours commonly include redness of the skin (erythema).

- Exposed persons will notice eye irritation, perhaps burning on the skin, or effects of upper airway irritation.

- There may be reddening in the conjunctiva (mild conjunctivitis – eye infection).

- The patient may have upper respiratory complaints such as aching sinuses, sore throat, fits, cardiac arrhythmias and convulsions. These may progress gradually depending on the amount of exposure.

Protection and decontamination

- Mustard gas may penetrate clothing, including leather, therefore full PPE must be worn, including full respiratory protection in contaminated areas or when handling casualties.

- Due to off-gassing (re-evaporation), casualties should be transported in such a way that emergency personnel do not become contaminated or exposed to fumes.

- Eye decontamination: wash with plenty of water or saline (salty) water for at least 15 minutes.

- Skin decontamination: avoid showering the victim as this may spread the threat. Apply powder (talcum powder or flour). If this is not available, wash exposed area thoroughly with soapy water, using the rinse–wipe–rinse method.

- Activated charcoal is of unproven benefit, but may be used.

First aid

- PPE-protected first responder emergency personnel should undertake physical examinations, remembering that mustard gas exposure may result in no immediate physical signs.

- The first responder should note and set aside for further observation any people who might have been exposed to this agent's liquid or vapour.

- Decontamination of the liquid from skin and eyes must be performed immediately if damage is to be prevented or lessened.

Case management

- Patients should be kept in an area where they may be observed carefully for any deterioration in medical condition.

- Use of antibiotics and analgaesia are recommended.

- If there are large burns, apply Fuller's earth.

- Administer symptomatic and supportive care as required – support breathing and circulation.

- If symptoms improve, or patient has not deteriorated within 24 hours, then casualties should be discharged with information on criteria to seek further medical advice.

- For severe cases, admit to an intensive care unit or equivalent wards. Oxygen with humidification may be required for respiratory distress. Ventilate if necessary.

- Monitor white blood cell count – an initial rise may lead to significant fall.

[Source: HPA, 2003.]

Phosphine

Key characteristics

- Phosphine is a colourless, flammable gas with a characteristic odour described as garlic or decaying fish; the odour threshold does not provide sufficient warning of dangerous concentrations.

- Aluminium phosphide reacts with water to release phosphine.

- Risk of cross-contamination.

Effects, including signs and symptoms

- Exposure to high concentration of phosphine leads to profound hypotension, collapse and death.

- Acute clinical effects: initially there may be a dry thirst, muscle pain, chills, cough, tight chest, headache, fatigue, dizziness, failure of muscle coordination, and confusion.

- Systemic effects may occur, including tremor, paraesthesia, diplopia, respiratory failure and coma.

- Inhalation: results in severe respiratory tract irritation. Following inhalation death may be sudden, usually occurring within four days, but may be delayed for 1–2 weeks.

- Ingestion: may lead to local mucosal irritation, pain in upper and middle region of abdomen, nausea, vomiting, diarrhoea, swelling of the lips, mouth and larynx and abdominal pain. Severe clinical effects may be delayed for up to a week.

- Eye exposure: it is thought that phosphine may cause irritation, lacrimation (tears) and conjunctivitis, although few data are available.

- Skin exposure: sweating, cyanosis (a bluish discoloration of skin and mucus membrane due to excessive concentration of reduced haemoglobin in the blood) and skin irritation may occur.

- Restlessness and anxiety are common following ingestion of aluminium phosphide.

Protection and decontamination

- Rescuers should ideally be trained personnel and must be careful not to put themselves at risk, and should wear full PPE and breathing apparatus in the event of a large spillage.

- Stay upwind and out of low areas, and ventilate closed spaces.

resource four

139

- Skin exposure: remove contaminated clothing, if possible under a soapy water shower, and place in double, sealed, clear (labelled) plastic bags; store bags in a secure area away from patients and staff.

First aid

- Terminate exposure and support vital functions.

- The casualty should be moved to an uncontaminated area.

- If casualty is unconscious a clear airway should be established and maintained; give 100 per cent oxygen if available.

- If the patient stops breathing, expired air resuscitation should be started immediately using a pocket mask with a one-way valve, if available. Where the face is contaminated, expired air resuscitation should not be attempted unless an airway with rescuer protection is used.

Case management

Inhalation exposure

- If respiratory irritation occurs, assess respiratory function and, if necessary, perform chest X-ray to check for chemical pneumonia.

- Maintain a clear airway, give humidified oxygen and ventilate if necessary.

- Consider the use of steroids to reduce the inflammatory response.

Skin exposure

- Wash the skin thoroughly with plenty of soapy water.

Eye exposure

- Irrigate thoroughly with water or saline water for 15 minutes.

- Encourage small quantities of oral fluids (no more than 50–100 ml in total) unless perforation is suspected.

[Source: adapted from HPA, 2003.]

Lewisite

Key characteristics

- Industrially produced lewisite is an amber to dark brown liquid with a strong, penetrating geranium odour. The pure compound is a colourless, odourless, oily liquid.

- Routes of exposure include inhalation, or absorption following skin or eye contact.

- Lewisite is a severe irritant, and contact with the vapour or liquid can be fatal.

Effects, including signs and symptoms

- Lewisite produces immediate effects. The vapour of this chemical causes effects similar to those of riot-control agents (burning or pain in eyes, exposed mucous membranes and skin) producing severe pain, which increases after the patient has been in the fresh air.

- Signs of tissue destruction and death will be manifest within minutes.

- Inhalation: exposure to lewisite vapour causes severe respiratory tract irritation and inflammation (damaging the respiratory tract epithelium) after a latency period of a few hours, and may cause death. Common symptoms are immediate burning pain, runny nose and violent sneezing, cough and frothing mucous, fluid in the lungs.

- Skin: absorption may occur after contact with lewisite liquid or vapour. Immediate stinging pain, skin redness within 30 minutes, with pain and itching for 24 hours, blisters within 12 hours with pain lasting two to three days, deep skin burns.

- Eyes: absorption may occur after contact with lewisite liquid or vapour. The agent acts within minutes, with instant pain on contact, irritation, swelling of the conjunctiva and eyelids, iritis and corneal scarring. Permanent damage or blindness within one minute in high doses.

- Systemic absorption may also occur. Poisoning can cause restlessness, weakness, subnormal temperature and low blood pressure, non-fatal destruction of the blood causing anaemia, liver damage, shock and death.

Protection and decontamination

- Staff involved should wear full PPE.

- Remove the casualty/victim from the source of exposure, then remove contaminated clothing.

- Avoid showering the victim as this may spread the threat.

resource four

First aid

- Survey the extent of injury. Avoid skin contact at all times.
- Treat affected skin with Fuller's earth or soapy water for decontamination.
- Immediately flush eyes with saline water for 15 minutes.

Case management

- Treat pulmonary/severe effects with oxygen if necessary, and give pain relievers.
- With severe poisoning, do not induce vomiting. Give patients milk or clean water to drink.

[Source: WHO 2001.]

Decontamination procedures for victims of chemical contamination

Principles of decontamination

The aim of decontamination is to remove pathogenic organisms from a person or object, to reduce the number of active organisms to an insignificant level. Washing with soapy water should remove 99.9 per cent of organisms.

Preparations for treatment

If a chemical or biological agent such as anthrax is released in a building, the people and contents must be decontaminated as soon as possible.

- All casualties/victims, whether injured or not, who are exiting the hot zone should be suspected of being contaminated and undergo a decontamination process.

- If exposed members of the beneficiary population have life-threatening injuries or illness, they must be stabilized before decontamination takes place.

- Decontamination should be accomplished before admission to a ward or elsewhere in the medical facility, or another building.

Decontamination of chemical and biological agents

Generally, vapour from nerve agents, cyanide and phosgene does not penetrate the skin. Mustard vapour can damage skin, but by the time a casualty reaches the decontamination area it will have evaporated or have been absorbed into the skin and hair. Mass decontamination in the event of a biological agent disease outbreak is not likely to be useful, except in the case of ricin toxins. People who were not in the immediate area, but are still at risk of contracting disease in a downwind hazard, do not need physical decontamination as the level of organisms would be low.

Personal protective equipment (PPE) for mass decontamination

Mass decontamination of exposed victims should take place in the warm zone on the outer edge of the contaminated area, by trained persons wearing full PPE. Therefore, unless NGOs have full PPE at hand they should not carry out direct decontamination of victims of chemical, biological or radiation incidents.

Decontamination procedures

■ People fleeing a chemical incident may reach an area where they are out of danger, but they may still have chemical substance contamination on their skin and clothes. Off-gassing (re-evaporation) of toxic vapours from the substance can be dangerous for the person helping, therefore caution should be taken in assisting individuals until they have been decontaminated.

■ As a precaution for possible off-gassing, or suspicion of non-decontamination of affected people, mass decontamination assistance would require the donning of PPE. The sight of helpers wearing such outfits may cause further alarm and distress among the affected population. Panic and looting may also pose a security risk.

■ A number of staff would be required to assist in channelling men, women and children separately through a decontamination process, as this must be carried out in pairs, and PPE would have to be changed after a short period according to the specific instructions.

PPE kits for decontamination systems

Standard precautions to limit exposure to contaminants include the use of PPE. The kit is described in Box V.1.

Decontamination bathing equipment and materials kits are listed in Box V.2.

Decontamination areas would require:

■ Provision of enclosures – separate bathing or shower tents for men and women, to allow privacy appropriate to the culture.

■ People to undress, shower or wash the whole body and to dress in clean or temporary clothing.

■ Set-up of a decontamination area for those unable to walk (litter casualties). This comprises several litter stands for sequential patient transfer.

■ Set-up of another area for injured people who are able to walk (ambulatory casualties) but require assistance.

Box V.1   PPE for decontamination process

■ Gas-tight suits with face masks and respirators, the level depending on the type and concentration of the chemical agent.

■ Butyl rubber gloves, boots (or shoe covers), rubber aprons, overalls.

■ Replacement or temporary clothing.

■ Arrangements for double-bagging and disposal of contaminated clothing.

Box V.2 PPE equipment

- Shower unit or hosepipes.

- Bathing tent, divided into three or four parts for derobing, washing, and robing.

- Lightweight stretcher trestles.

- Soap, buckets (5–10 litres capacity), sponges, soft brushes; bleach for materials and objects.

- Generators to pump water and copious amounts of water.

Water requirements

- Use clean, uncontaminated water supplies from sealed containers or brought in from safe locations (e.g. in tankers): the exact amount needed to decontaminate a person will depend on body size, type and degree of contamination: allow 10–20 litres per person.

- Standard procedures for guiding water source selection, analysis and storage should be observed (Sphere Project, 2003).

- Vulnerability assessment of water sources should be conducted where there is a risk of chemical, biological or radiation contamination.

- There are no field kits available to screen water quality for biological pathogens accurately and rapidly. Some military forces may possess water-testing devices for certain chemical agents and radioactive contamination.

- Water purification procedures involve filtration and chlorination methods to reduce chemical and biological waterborne hazards and contamination.

- Ground water, unless contaminated with run-off contaminants, would be the safest source of water supply. Surface water is less protected. Additional water supplies should be accessed from local authorities or through the aid community.

- Cold water encourages the pores of the skin to close and so reduces chemical absorption. Disadvantages of using cold water are the possibility of thermal shock and hypothermia in aged, frail, very young and traumatized people. Lukewarm water should be considered for these people if possible.

Decontamination process

- Mass decontamination would require drenching and flushing the agent from the skin with low-pressure water sprays, followed by use of the rinse–wipe–rinse method on an individual, before admission to a health structure.

resource five

- Pumps and hoses would have to be set up to create a large shower 'corridor' in a paved area, for contaminated people to pass through. If facilities exist, fire sprinkler systems could be utilized.

Individual decontamination procedures

People who are capable of decontaminating themselves should do so under supervision and instruction, as follows.

Stage 1

- Prepare a mild soapy solution with 5 ml soap per litre of water.
- Carefully remove contaminated clothing from head to foot (but not over the head; cutting the clothing if the casualty is injured and taking care not to spread contamination from clothing to skin), or remove just the outer layers of clothing and shoes.
- Contaminated clothing should be placed in double bags, tagged, and removed to a remote section of the medical facility to avoid creating a hazard from a concentration of contamination.
- The clothing should be decontaminated or disposed of by qualified personnel and protected as time permits.

Stage 2

- The second phase of decontamination consists of washing or wiping the patient's face, hands and any other parts of the body which were exposed to the agent. This should leave the patient 98 per cent decontaminated.

Stage 3

- The third phase consists of washing the hair, or clipping the hair and washing the scalp (without the water run-off touching the face). This phase need be accomplished only if the person arrives without headgear and/or monitoring indicates that the hair is contaminated.

[Source: Adapted from NATO 2001.]

Walking wounded (ambulatory casualties) and self-decontamination

In the warm zone (out of hazard danger area), from a safe distance give instructions to the casualty as follows.

- Remove any immediate signs of substances on the skin by scraping or sweeping the material away. Remove all personal items, such as a watch or jewellery, from the body.

- If spectacles have to be worn, first soak them in hypochlorite (5 per cent diluted chlorine) solution for five minutes.

- Flush eyes with large amounts of clean water.

- Wash face and hair with soap and water, and rinse. Avoid contact with eyes, nostrils and ears.

- Remove outer clothing by pulling it away from the body without touching the skin.

- Label clothing and personal property with the individual's name.

- Double-bag contaminated clothing, which should be treated as hazardous waste, and place in a controlled area until it can be decontaminated or disposed of.

- Rinse exposed skin, starting from the neck down, with a soapy water solution. Do not swab or wipe with a cloth.

- Wipe the affected areas with a wet sponge or brush.

- Rinse with clean, lukewarm or cold water; use showers if available.

- Repeat the process if skin contamination remains obvious.

Contaminated clothing

- Fresh clothing or a blanket wrap would be required.

- Contaminated clothing should first be disinfected in a chlorine solution and then washed with detergent.

- Contaminated disposable personal protective clothing (PPE) should be double plastic bagged before disposal.

Injured or unconscious casualties (litter patient decontamination)

To be performed by PPE-protected emergency medical personnel only:

- Remove any obvious contaminants from the skin.

- Remove personal property and clothing (cut away from the skin).

- Transfer to a stretcher or litter with a plastic sheeting cover.

resource five

- Blot the casualty's skin (not the face) with a solution of soapy water.

- Flush superficial wounds with the solution and apply new dressings.

- Saturate any splints and the skin underneath with soapy water.

- Wash with copious amounts of clean water, starting with face and hands downwards.

- Transfer to the support area for equipping with clean clothing or blankets.

Monitoring (to check that no further residual contamination exits)

- Only personnel wearing PPE should monitor the person, with a chemical agent monitor if available.

- When confirmed as clear of any chemical contaminant, transfer the person over a control line by passing from the warm to the cold zone (the clean and safe area).

- Wash PPE (apron and gloves) in 5 per cent hypochlorite solution before the patient is transferred to another clean stretcher.

Triage

Only after decontamination can medical screening procedures take place in the cold zone.

Transfer the patient to a medical facility. Ambulances or vehicles transporting patients who are not completely free from contaminants must be decontaminated before they can be used by clean patients.

Decontamination of equipment

- Physically contaminated equipment and rooms should be decontaminated.

- Aeration outdoors in wind and sunlight for several days should decontaminate articles which are slightly affected or contaminated by vapour.

- Soapy water heated to just below boiling point can be used to soak heavily contaminated items for one hour, followed by a rinse in cold water, then dry.

- Slurry solution (30 per cent aqueous slurry of bleach) can be sprayed onto items of clothing, or applied by broom or swab to equipment immediately after contamination, then washed off with water. For wood litter, leave for 12–24 hours.

- For metal stretchers and all contaminated surfaces, decontaminate with bleach slurry or flush with hot soapy water, leave for 30 minutes, flush with water, and aerate outdoors for several hours.

- Boil nylon and canvas bags for one hour in soapy water, rinse and air-dry.
- Soak shoes, straps and leather equipment in water heated to 50–55°C (122–133°F) for 4–6 hours, then air-dry.

Decontamination of buildings

In buildings, sufficient contamination may be transferred from room to room via air-conditioning systems and movement of people. Intake ducts and vents should be closed, and the inner walls and contents of the room washed with 5 per cent chlorine solution.

Contaminated waste disposal

For the safety of sanitation workers, precautions should be taken against the risk of secondary contamination. Standards of precautions (use of face masks, shoe covers, gloves, gowns and eye protection) should be observed.

- If involved, NGOs would need to establish strict medical waste-disposal protocols.
- Contaminated water: special collection in water barrels, and disposal of run-off, should be a minimum of two metres away from underground water sources and densely populated areas.
- Discharge of CBR contaminated wastes into sewage systems can create a serious health risk, but dilution would significantly reduce the persistence of the substance.
- The excreta of radioactively or chemically contaminated individuals would not pose greater than normal health risks.
- Contaminated water run-off from vesicant agents, such as mustard gas, would gradually turn to sludge and degrade over time.
- Medical waste, such as used needles, should be placed in sealed plastic containers and clearly labelled, and disposed of in a sharps pit or burned.
- Contaminated clothing, placed in plastic bags, should be stored in closed, airtight containers, or covered with earth to prevent the escape of toxic vapours in a marked place over 73 metres downwind of the decontamination area.
- Contaminated body disposal: incineration destroys a high percentage of infectious microorganisms of a biological agent.
- Burial: if the body of a victim is to be buried, special mortuary facilities or a demarcated burial site with a deep grave would have to be found in a secure area at a safe distance from habitation sites and water sources.
- Chemical and radioactive waste should not be incinerated as it can produce explosions, potentially toxic airborne chemical emissions, and airborne radioactive contamination.

resource five

Extreme Emergencies

- Sanitary landfill is only effective using liners to prevent ground water contamination, and ensuring security to prevent scavenging of waste material.

- Vector control measures may be necessary where CBR contamination is suspected to minimize the health risk of infectious disease transmission and vector breeding grounds, especially in the event of weaponized biological agents such as plague and tularaemia.

- The use of mass insecticides against a biological agent outbreak must be weighed against the chemical risks and the potential for vector-borne disease.

Medical protocols for key biological agents (emerging infectious diseases)

Anthrax

Key characteristics

To be treated as a case of deliberate release unless an alternative cause is positively established.

- Anthrax is caused by the bacteria *Bacillus anthracis*.

- It naturally affects grazing animals such as sheep, cattle and goats.

- It affects the skin, guts or lungs, depending on how the bacteria entered the body.

- In a bioterrorist attack it can enter the body by inhalation – this is potentially fatal.

- It can be transmitted from person to person by direct inhalation. It is not an airborne contagious disease (not transmitted through the air).

Incubation period

The incubation period depends on many factors, such as the amount of anthrax inhaled. It can be as short as two days or as long as 60 days.

Signs and symptoms

- The symptoms are different depending on the type of anthrax.

- **Cutaneous**: a small sore that develops into a blister. The blister then develops into an ulcer with a black area in the centre. The sore does not hurt. Lips and hands may go blue with rapid deterioration.

- **Gastrointestinal**: the first symptoms are nausea, loss of appetite, bloody diarrhoea and fever, followed by bad stomach pain.

- **Inhalation**: flu-like symptoms (lasting two to four days) are the first sign of inhalation of anthrax, and include a sore throat, mild fever and muscle aches.

Later symptoms include a cough, chest discomfort, and shortness of breath, tiredness and muscle aches.

Diagnosis

- Typical appearance on the X-ray.

- Blood test may also help two to three days after onset.

Protection and decontamination

- Clothes of affected persons should be removed, bagged and disposed of by someone wearing gloves, gown and respiratory protection.

- The exposed person should shower thoroughly with soapy water.

- Exposed environmental surfaces may be cleaned with soapy water or chlorine solution.

Vaccination

There is a preventive vaccine against anthrax, but it is recommended only for those at risk from occupational exposure. Vaccination is not recommended for the general public. There should be no risks to carers of catching the disease. In deliberate release, an individual risk is assessed on a case-by-case basis. Post-exposure prophylaxis with antibiotics can be very effective in preventing disease, if given early enough.

Case management

- The more quickly the treatment starts, the better. If sure of exposure, start treatment before any flu-like symptoms occur.

- Once anthrax disease is established, treatment is by injection into the vein (intravenous route).

- A course of three vaccinations over six weeks is necessary to accompany the treatment prior to symptoms.

- Use of antibiotics: first choice, Ciprofloxacin (not licensed for prescription to pregnant women or children); second choice, Benzylpenicillin or Doxycycline.

- In cases of gastrointestinal and pulmonary infection, provide intensive care in addition to antibiotic therapy.

[Sources: HPA, 2003; USA Department of Health and Human Services; US Centers for Disease Control and Prevention.]

Smallpox

Key characteristics

- Smallpox virus exists in two forms: variola minor and variola major. The latter is more contagious, and has a mortality rate that is 0.3 per cent greater in the unvaccinated.

- The naturally occurring virus infection was eradicated in 1977. Stocks of variola remained and could potentially be used as a biological weapon.

- Transmission occurs person-to-person: infected people can spread the disease from the moment the fever has begun until the last scabs fall off (three weeks).

Incubation period

The incubation period is between seven and 17 days (usually 10–16 days), although the individual may look and feel healthy.

Signs and symptoms

- Fever, systemic toxicity, rash, lesions occurring at the same time and stage of development.

- Acute manifestations with malaise, fever, rigors, vomiting, abdominal pain, headache and backache.

- Small red spots appear on the tongue and in mouth, they develop into sores that break open and spread large amounts of virus in the mouth and throat (a patient is most contagious at this time).

- Within 24 hours a rash appears on the face: spreading to the arms and then to the hands and feet, it quickly progresses from macules to papules (small, circumscribed, solid, elevated lesions of the skin). This progressive distribution is a distinctive diagnostic feature of smallpox.

- By day 4, spots fill with thick fluid and have a dent in the centre, which is a major distinguishing feature, and fever reappears.

- By 8–14 days after the onset of symptoms, scabs form on the spots which, when they fall off, leave depressed scars.

Diagnosis

Diagnostic samples include pharyngeal (throat) swabs, scab material, serum.

Protection and decontamination

- Strict infection control precautions are required. Carers, medical personnel, health attendants and mortuary workers (even if vaccinated) should wear full personal protective equipment (PPE: gloves, gown, eye protection, face mask) to guard against airborne transmission.

- Isolate the patient within a specialist isolation hospital. If necessary, establish a separate unit.

- Shower the patient using soapy water or antiseptic liquid soap.

- Use a very diluted solution of household bleach to clean the environment.

- Wash all clothes, bed linen and towels in hot water, detergent and disinfectant such as bleach.

- Deceased bodies of smallpox cases should be buried deeply (at least two metres) and covered completely with powdered lime (calcium hydroxide) followed by soil.

Vaccination

Post-exposure vaccination is recommended (live-virus vaccine).

Case management

- Treat each symptom.

- Antivirals for use against smallpox are under investigation.

Any confirmed cases of smallpox should be considered an international emergency and treated as a case of deliberate release, with an immediate report made to the public health authorities.

[Sources: adapted from WHO Guidelines on Smallpox; HPA, 2003.]

Plague (bubonic plague)

Key characteristics

- Acute bacterial infection caused by *Yersinia pestis*.

- It infects rodents, cats and humans and is transmitted to humans by fleas or by direct contact with plague-infected animals. Tissues or body fluids of a plague-infected animal are highly infectious. Found particularly in Africa, Asia and south-west USA.

- It can affect the skin, blood or lungs, resulting in three types of plague: bubonic, pneumonic and septicaemic.

Incubation period

From exposure to bacteria to the development of initial symptoms takes from one to six days, most commonly two to four days.

Signs and symptoms

- **Bubonic plague** – when transmitted by the flea, a swelling of lymph nodes (buboe) occurs usually on the groin, underarms or neck, and spreads to the blood (septicaemia) and to the lung (pulmonary).

- **Pneumonic plague** – at first, flu-like symptoms with fever, headache and chills, progressing to pneumonia with cough, shortness of breath and chest pain. This form would be the most likely following a deliberate release. Person-to-person transmission can occur.

- **Septicaemia plague** – occurs when plague bacteria multiply in the blood. This can be by the action of pneumonic or bubonic plague, or it can occur by itself. When it occurs alone, it is caused in the same mechanism as bubonic plague. Patients have fever, chills, prostration, abdominal pain, shock, and bleeding into skin and other organs. Septicaemic plague does not spread from person to person.

- It is possible for a sufferer to transmit infection up to 72 hours after the start of treatment.

Diagnosis

- *Yersinia pestis* is a small, Gram-negative coccibacillus; from clinical specimens it may appear pleomorphic (occurs in various distinct forms).

- Can be confirmed by testing sputum or blood. This may take one or two days. The chest X-ray would appear abnormal.

Protection and decontamination

■ All frontline staff must use PPE.

■ Decontaminate by showering; all clothing must be double-bagged or destroyed.

Vaccination

■ Plague vaccine exists, but not for routine use. It should be considered only for high-risk professionals.

Case management

■ Prevent secondary cases, and ensure access to a complete course of preventive treatment.

■ Ensure those who may be developing the disease are identified and managed appropriately.

■ Provided the disease is identified in its early stages, it can be treated very effectively with antibiotics: first choice, Gentamicin (3–5 mg/kg/day as three doses intravenously, slowly, 3 minutes); second choice, Streptomycin (1 g intramuscularly, twice daily); third choice, Ciprofloxacin (400 mg intravenously, twice a day). For mild cases: Doxycycline (100 mg orally twice a day); or Streptomycin (15 mg/kg/day intramuscularly, twice daily).

■ Patients or cases of plague pneumonia should be nursed in a single room, with the door closed wherever possible. All persons entering the room should wear surgical masks and aprons/gowns.

■ Strict isolation, with airborne precaution, is needed in the event of pneumonic plague.

■ **Once a case is suspected the local health authorities must be informed immediately.**

[Source: adapted from Department of Health, 2001; HPA, 2003; de Jong and Prosser, 2003.]

Brucellosis (or brucella)

Key characteristics

- Brucellosis is a bacterial disease which has a natural reservoir in different animals (cattle, camels, swine and dogs).

- Transmission: acquired by humans via the oral route through ingestion of unpasteurized milk, cheese and dairy products or contaminated meat; or via inhalation of aerosols generated on farms and slaughterhouses; or via inhalation of aerosols or dusts that contain organisms; or via inoculation of abraded skin, mucosal surfaces or skin lesions in persons having close contact with animals.

- Intentional exposure would probably involve aerosolization, and could involve contamination of foodstuffs.

Incubation period

- Incubation period varies from five days to eight weeks, usually two to eight weeks.

- Duration of illness, weeks to months.

- No person-to-person transmission.

Signs and symptoms

- Onset may be sudden (50 per cent) or develop gradually (50 per cent).

- Non-specific symptoms or fever, malaise, fatigue, weight loss, chills, sweating, depression and mental changes may occur.

- Illness persists as a systemic illness, without localizing signs and symptoms.

- Fever can be intermittent. Pulmonary infection, genito-urinary tract inflammation, cardiovascular problems (endocarditis), neurological disorders (meningitis [rare], depression, fatigue, headache).

Diagnosis

- Appropriate isolation of the infectious agent from blood, bone marrow or other tissues.

- Serological tests are useful, but are difficult to interpret in chronic disease.

Vaccination

- No vaccine is available for human use.

Protection and decontamination

- Healthcare workers should observe standard precaution procedures.
- Personal decontamination with soapy water for 10–15 minutes.

Case management

- Isolate the infected person(s) in a side room.
- Post exposure: give Doxycycline (100 mg twice a day) plus Rifampicin (600–900 mg/day) orally for 6 weeks; or Doxycycline (100 mg twice a day for 6 weeks) plus Streptomycin (1 g/day intramuscularly for 2 weeks).
- Prolonged treatment is necessary if there are organ complications (as listed above).

Case fatality is less than 2 per cent. Untreated brucellosis may result in severe morbidity for months or years.

[Source: WHO 2001.]

Viral haemorrhagic fevers

Key characteristics

- These are groups of illnesses caused by several distinct families of viruses; some cause relatively mild illness, while others cause severe, life-threatening illness.

- These viruses are endemic in Africa, South America and Asia. Recent outbreaks of Ebola infection have occurred in West Africa.

- They could be released as an aerosol in a bioterrorism attack.

- The viruses are not highly infectious from person to person (that is, they are not communicable).

- For contamination to take place, contact with body fluid is necessary.

Incubation period

- The incubation period is rarely longer than 21 days.

Signs and symptoms

- Symptoms vary according to the type of virus, but initial symptoms include: fever, fatigue, dizziness, muscle aches and weakness. Severely ill patients may show signs of bleeding under the skin, from body orifices such as the mouth, eyes and ears, or into internal organs.

- Severely ill patients may also show signs of shock, kidney failure and nervous system malfunction, including coma, delirium and seizures.

Diagnosis

- It is often difficult to distinguish viral haemorrhagic fevers clinically from each other, and from severe malaria, yellow fever and septicaemia.

- Definitive diagnosis requires testing that is available only in highly specialized laboratories.

- Laboratory specimens may be biohazardous and must be handled with extreme care at the highest level of biosafety containment.

Protection and decontamination

- Medical care-givers, persons taking care of the sick, health attendants and mortuary workers, even if vaccinated, should wear full PPE, including double gloves, impermeable gowns, leg and shoe coverings, face shields/goggles for eye protection, and masks or respirators (for airborne precautions).

- Isolate the patient.

resource six

- Use a very diluted solution of soapy water.

- Wash all clothes, bed linen and towels in hot water and disinfectant (bleach).

- If facilities are available, patients should be nursed in a negative-pressure isolation room.

- Bodies of haemorrhagic fever virus victims should be buried deeply (at least two metres) and completely covered with powdered lime (calcium hydroxide).

Vaccination

- A vaccine is available for yellow fever, and is recommended to those travelling to endemic areas. No vaccines are available against other types of haemorrhagic fever viruses.

Case management

- Some can be treated with antiviral drugs, e.g. Ribavirin is potentially effective for Lassa fever/Congo Crimean Haemorrhagic Fever (CCHF)/arena viruses; when used with Interferon, infections can be managed.

- **Once a case has been identified, the local health authorities must be informed immediately.**

[Source: WHO 2001.]

Tularaemia
Key characteristics

- Tularaemia is caused by a highly infectious bacterium. The bacteria naturally inhabit small mammals such as voles, mice, water rats, squirrels, rabbits and hares.

- Natural transmission is by infected insects such as ticks or deerflies, or by handling infectious animal tissues or fluids.

- Transmission is also via direct contact or ingestion of contaminated water, food, or oil; or by breathing in bacteria from dust or aerosols.

Incubation period

- In humans, the incubation period is typically three to five days with a range of one to 14 days.

Signs and symptoms

- Clinical manifestations relate to the route of introduction and the virulence of the disease agent.

- There may be indolent ulcers at the introduction site and swollen lymph nodes.

- Ingestion may lead to pharyngitis, abdominal pain, vomiting and diarrhoea.

- Inhalation may lead to lung infection, especially in the pleural spaces.

- Eye infections are rare but can result in purulent conjunctivitis.

Diagnosis

- Clinical diagnosis is common. Confirm by a rise in specific serum antibodies usually appearing in the second week of disease. Examination of ulcer exudates or lymph node aspirates by Fast Acid test may provide a rapid diagnosis.

Protection and decontamination

- Isolation is not recommended for tularaemia patients, given that there is no established human-to-human transmission.

- Post-exposure prophylaxis with antibiotics may be recommended in some instances. Doxycycline or Ciprofloxacin, daily for 14 days, have been recommended for persons thought to have had an infectious exposure.

resource six

Vaccination

■ A live vaccine is available in some countries for limited use only, and has been used to protect laboratory staff who routinely work with bacteria.

Case management

■ Tularaemia is best treated with the antibiotics Streptomycin or Gentamicin – given by injection daily for 10 days.

■ Alternative antibiotics include tetracycline (such as Doxycycline) or Chloramphenicol daily for 14 days, which can be given by injection or by mouth.

■ Fluoroquinolones, such as Ciprofloxacin, have been used with success and may be given by injection or by mouth.

■ **Once a case has been established or is suspected, the local health authorities must be informed immediately.**

[Sources: WHO 2001; WHO-EMRO 2003.)

Civil nuclear site incidents

Alerting procedures

The operators of all the major civil nuclear sites should have plans for dealing with any nuclear emergency scenarios that can reasonably be foreseen. In the event of a hazardous condition causing a radiological hazard to the public in the vicinity of the site, the senior manager present on the site should declare an **off-site emergency** and should invoke the site emergency plan.

For a less hazardous condition, the effect of which is confined to within the site security fence, an **on-site emergency** or **site incident** would be declared. A site emergency controller should set up a series of notification chains so that all relevant organizations, local emergency teams and national bodies are quickly informed of the emergency.

Overseas nuclear accident

The first notification of an overseas nuclear accident is likely to be received by the International Atomic Energy Agency's (IAEA) Convention on Early Notification of a Nuclear Accident. Alternatively, notification may come via another member state of the European Union through the EU rapid notification procedures.

Other nuclear accidents

If an accident occurs at a military or defence establishment, or involving nuclear weapons in transit, the national Ministry of Defence should be in the lead and should alert other government departments.

The national transport ministry should inform the national health ministry of any civil transport accidents involving nuclear material which have any major radiological consequences.

Advice and information

Measures should be taken to protect the public:

- sheltering

- evacuation

- issuing of potassium iodate tablets

- restrictions on agricultural products

- restrictions on water

- personal monitoring arrangements

- travel restrictions

- need for additional resources.

Coordination

A government body should be the focal point for coordination of central government actions throughout the emergency.

Action

Primarily decontamination of contaminated members of the public, casualties and widespread use of stable iodine prophylaxis.

Potassium iodate

- The likelihood of an incident involving the release of radioactivity which includes radioiodine (a fission product produced only in nuclear reactors or nuclear explosions), which is sufficiently widespread to involve stable iodine as a significant countermeasure for a national population, is extremely low. (Nuclear installations already have emergency plans to cover scenarios with more local contamination.)

- Stockpiles of potassium iodate tablets are focused on areas close to nuclear installations and on the members of the population most at risk from the health detriments of radioiodine (thyroid disease): those under 40, and particularly infants and young children. Downwind from a nuclear accident or detonation, most casualties result from radioactive iodine poisoning of the thyroid gland. Children are the highest-risk group.

- Potassium iodide protects thyroid from radioactive poisoning. If taken before exposure it reduces the threat by 95 per cent.

Stable iodine prophylaxis recommended dosages would be: adults, two (100 mg) tablets; children 3–12 years, one tablet; children 1 month–3 years, half a tablet; newborn infants, quarter of a tablet.

RESOURCE VIII
Training and capacity building

Building knowledge and understanding of CBRNE hazards and contaminants into organizational policy would improve NGOs' capacity to protect both staff and civilian populations. Using a modular, incremental step approach, an introduction to the key agents and hazards, their immediate effects, and mitigation and protective measures could be built on with further modules relevant to staff roles. Training healthcare workers in the recognition and initial management of both biological and chemical casualties is also recommended.

Training objectives

The main objectives of training should be to:

- familiarize field staff and healthcare workers with the acute consequences of a CBRNE incident

- train staff to recognize general symptoms of chemical and radiation exposure

- teach field triage principles in the context of an incident

- review the initial management of CBR victims

- enhance understanding of the role NGOs can play in emergency response to a CBRNE incident.

Curriculum components

CBRNE threats (prevention, treatment and containment of effects and injuries).

Chemical

- What is a chemical weapon?

- Important features of chemical weapons

- Chemical versus biological weapons

- Chemical agent properties and dispersal systems

- Classification of chemical agents

- Classes of chemical agents
- Nerve agents – health effects and treatment
- Blister agents (mustard gas) – health effects and treatment
- Choking agents (phosphine)
- Blood agents (cyanide) – health effects and treatment
- Other agents – incapacitating, tearing and vomiting agents
- Industrial hazards – chemical threats
- Protection
- Detection devices
- Personal protective equipment (PPE)
- Treatment
- Decontamination
- Liquids used for decontamination
- Decontamination zones
- Medical countermeasures (antidotes and vaccines)

Biological

- What is a biological weapon?
- Use of biological weapons
- Types of biological agent (skin, lungs)
- Classification – anthrax, smallpox, Ebola and haemorrhagic fever viruses, plague, botulism, tularaemia, ricin, brucellosis
- Methods of diagnosis
- Mode of transmission
- Diagnosis
- Symptoms
- Treatment
- Containment

Radiation

Introduction

- What is radiation?
- What are sources of radiation?
- How is radiation measured?
- What does radioactive half-life mean?
- What does radioactive contamination mean?

Classification

- Types of radiation
- Nuclear weapons – overview
- Nuclear weapons – damage predictions
- What is a dirty bomb?
- What is depleted uranium?

Health effects

- How does radiation harm you?
- Major radiation accidents
- Acute radiation syndrome

Protection

- Protecting against radiation injury
- What to do after a radiological or nuclear explosion?
- Radiation detection
- Use of potassium iodate tablets

Treatment

- What can I do to help myself and others?
- Decontamination
- Treatment of acute radiation syndrome
- Internal contamination treatment

- Treatment priorities
- Psychological effects of radiation exposure
- Radiation threat instruction sheet

Early recognition: knowledge of early clinical signs

- Surveillance and data collection systems (sensitive to unusually high rates, also to unusual conditions; reporting forms)
- Personal safety and protection (before, during and after CBRNE exposure)
- Construction of safe rooms; techniques for sheltering in-place
- Decontamination techniques (individual and mass)
- Management of mass casualties
- Basic first aid
- Medical treatment and care of a casualty – management protocols
- Psychosocial care (culturally appropriate) – fear and anxiety among victims and the 'worried well'
- CBRNE profile awareness
- Identification of civil partners and structures for mass decontamination and treatment

[Sources: adapted from IMC/UCLA (2003) CD-ROM, with permission to duplicate for educational purposes.]

Training bodies and resource materials

The following is a summary of key agencies providing training resources that may be useful for NGOs who are seeking to build awareness and skills related to deliberate or accidental CBRNE incidents. Examples of organizations in the UK, USA and Canada are cited, although training establishments offering this type of training may also be found in other countries.

United Kingdom

Centurion Risk Services Ltd, UK

Centurion is a leading risk assessment and training company, providing training on practical hostile environments and first aid advice and instruction to journalists and emergency and humanitarian aid personnel working in hazardous regions. Centurion provides CBRNE tailored risk and security services for NGOs and others.

Web: www.centurion.co.uk

Chemical Hazards and Poisons Division, Health Protection Agency, UK

Provides one–day course on 'How to Respond to Chemical Incidents':

- understanding the role of public health in the management of chemical incidents

- awareness of the appropriate and timely response to chemical incidents

- understanding the interaction with other agencies involved in incident management.

Web: www.hpa.org.uk

MASC – Medical and Safety Consultants

MASC provides tailor-made courses specific to the needs of individuals and organizations working in remote and often resource-poor environments. Course topics include:

- risk assessment and crisis management for managers

- contingency planning and preparation

- emergency situation management for field staff

- medical support to overseas operations

- conventional and unconventional terrorism (chemical and biological agents)

- breakout of a communicable disease.

Web: www.mascts.com

Ozonelink Ltd, UK

Ozonelink has seasoned, world-class experts to assist organizations to deal with the threat of crises such as terrorism and disasters. The organization can develop programmes tailored to the specific requirements of their clients, and offers modular hands-on chemical, biological, radiological, and nuclear awareness-raising, exercizing with real products. Training courses include:

- CBRN Risk Assessment: an independent evacuation and shelter risk assessment

- CBRN Basic Training: designed to give knowledge and confidence to work in urban environments unstable regions where CBRN weapons may be used

- Crisis Communication: a one–day media-handling course for CEOs and directors, includes public relations skills, crisis exercises, crisis message planning, crisis seminars and public relations strategy

- Training courses are one to three days, conducted on- or off-site, using client's and/or Ozone facilities.

Web: www.ozonelink.com

Pilgrims Group, Surrey, UK

Pilgrims' courses are developed for anyone travelling or working in regions of civil unrest, isolated fighting or all-out war. Originally developed for news media, these courses are also relevant to aid agencies. There are dedicated facilities in both the UK and the USA.

Services include international security risk management solutions, hostile environment and medical training, comprehensive one–day CBRN course.

Web: www.pilgrimsgroup.co.uk

Risk Lifesigns Group, UK

Risk Lifesigns provides tailor-made modular courses for organizations. Training programmes aim to help personnel acquire the knowledge and skills they need to become fully security aware, whatever their roles and countries of operation.

Training courses are suited to the needs of clients whose employees face open hostilities, such as aid workers or journalists. The training provided is related to CBR and tailored to risk and security services for NGOs.

Web: www.adventurelifesigns.co.uk/risk/chemical.php

International

Canadian Emergency Preparedness College, Canada

The College is leading the development of a comprehensive CBRN training programme for first responders, in collaboration with other federal departments and agencies including Health Canada and the Canadian Nuclear Safety Commission. It provides Canadian emergency institution expertise on CBRN for first responders at four levels: introductory, basic, intermediate and advanced. The course is structured to provide participants with a broad base from which to carry out emergency planning and operations as a member of an emergency site team.

Web: www.ocipep-bpiepc.gc.ca/ep/college/cepc_e.asp

Centers for Disease Control and Prevention (CDC), Atlanta, USA

CDC is recognized as the lead federal agency for protecting the health and safety of people in the USA and abroad. It is an agency of the Department of Health and Human Services.

Training programmes available include:

■ bioterrorism for national public health professionals

■ public health training on key emerging infectious diseases

■ online interactive training clinicians in diagnosis, treatment, recognition and prevention of bioterrorism agents.

Web: www.bt.cdc.gov

Centre of Excellence in Disaster Management and Humanitarian Assistance, USA

The Centre's mission is to promote effective civil–military management in international humanitarian assistance, disaster response and peacekeeping through education, training, research and information programmes.

The Centre offers customized education and training programmes for NGOs, designed to meet the specific training objectives of the requesting organization. The host organization selects the curriculum and develops a draft agenda based on the training objectives and target audience.

Web: www.coe-dmha.org

Center for International Health and Cooperation (CIHC), USA

The Center was founded in 1991 by a group of physicians and diplomats, to promote healing and peace in countries shattered by war, ethnic violence or natural disasters. CIHC is a leading humanitarian educational organization providing standard professional training, annual symposia, a variety of publications, and field assistance around the globe.

The Certificate Course in Disaster Management training is an intense one–week programme with all major aspects taught by an experienced faculty from the USA, Ireland, UK and Europe. The course includes modules on chemical weapons, biological weapons and nuclear disasters, and psychosocial health.

Web: www.cihc.org

Bioterrorism Library, Medical University of South Carolina (MUSC), USA

Medical University of South Carolina has a medical centre for the education of a broad range of health professionals, biomedical scientists and related personnel. Course topics include medical and healthcare information, biological warfare, bioterrorism and psychological aspects of bioterrorism.

Web: www.musc.edu

Training, Simulation and Performance Improvement, Southwest Research Institute, Texas, USA

Provides a modular chemical, biological, radiological and nuclear threats awareness course (also available on CD-ROM).

The Training Support Department offers courseware development, training resources support, computer-based training, simulation and performance improvement

Web: http://tspi.swri.org

US Army Medical Research Institute of Infectious Diseases (USAMRIID), Maryland, USA

USAMRIID conducts research to develop strategies, products, information, procedures and training programmes for medical defence against biological warfare threats and infectious diseases. It provides:

- in-house courses on medical management of chemical and biological casualties

- satellite series – live satellite education and training broadcasts to inform and educate healthcare professionals with detailed information on the most likely toxins terrorists might use.

Web: www.usamriid.army.mil

Training materials

South Carolina Prepares, USA

This site provides training and resources for public health preparedness, terrorism preparedness and disaster preparedness through a searchable database and links to relevant organizations and agencies. Training and resource topics covered include bioterrorism, chemical terrorism, agro-terrorism, water contamination, food contamination, man-made disasters, radiation/nuclear energy exposure, human disease control, animal disease control (e.g. West Nile Virus), and other emergency management or preparedness concerns.

Web: www.bioterrorism.library

Stockholm International Peace Research Institute, Free University Brussels and International Relations and Security Network

Educational Module on Chemical & Biological Weapons Nonproliferation, freely available online to improve knowledge and understanding of nonproliferation in general, and chemical and biological weapons in particular.

Web: http://cbw.sipri.se/

Training for Radiation Emergency Preparedness & Response

IAEA–WHO (2002) *Medical Preparedness and Response: Training for Radiation Emergency Preparedness & Response.* CD-ROM. Vienna: International Atomic Energy Agency. This CD-ROM provides 30 lectures (with 906 note pages) for five–day training courses for radiation emergency medical personnel, which includes topics on:

- detection of radiation and radioactive contamination

- biological effects of exposure to ionizing radiation

- deterministic and stochastic effects of radiation

- diagnosis and treatment of acute radiation syndrome

- diagnosis and treatment of radiation injuries

- cause and medical response in selected accidental cases

- major nuclear accidents: health consequences of Chernobyl nuclear accident

- radiation accidents: Iran, Peru, Estonia, Georgia, Turkey, Thailand

- criticality accidents: Russia, Japan

- psychological effects of long-term exposure and radiation injury

- overview of nuclear emergency preparedness and response

- planning the medical response to radiological accidents

- international cooperation for medical assistance to radiological accidents.

Web: www.who.int/

UN Disaster Management Training Programme (UNDMTP)

UNDMTP is developing a training module on 'Management of Preparedness and Response to Chemical, Biological and Radionuclear Incidents'. Existing training includes a range of modules, including:

- disaster preparedness, assessment, mitigation and management

- role and responsibilities of UN disaster management team.

Web: www.undmtp.org/modules.htm

WHO Health Action in Crisis

Provides training material on:

- technological disaster profiles
- terrorism and public health model
- chemical incidents
- preparedness for deliberate epidemics.

Web: www.who.int/health_topics/biological_weapons

Directory of organizations and conventions

Chemical hazards

Organisation for the Prohibition of Chemical Weapons (OPCW)

- The OPCW is the inter-state organization responsible for achieving the objectives of the Chemical Weapons Convention on the prohibition of use of the development, production and stockpiling of biological and toxin weapons and their destruction.

- OPCW proposes policies for the implementation of the Convention to member states and develops and delivers programmes with them.

- On a request for international assistance, OPCW provides protection and assistance to states against chemical weapons through its access to a package of international assistance measures. Resources can also be made available to non-member states if a request directed to the UN Secretary General is approved.

- OPCW can mobilize a response system consisting of an Advanced Coordination and Assessment Team (ACAT), which endeavours to arrive at the affected site within 3–12 hours to assess requirements and mobilize international assistance. Teams can also be made available by member states to provide detection equipment, decontamination equipment, field hospitals, medical antidotes and treatments, medical staff, and necessary infrastructure support for assistance operations.

- OPCW has a programme for the establishment of permanent stockpiles of protective equipment.

- In the case of an alleged use of chemical weapons, a state party may request the OPCW to conduct an investigation to collect facts.

Web: www.opcw.org

Euro-Atlantic Disaster Response Unit (EADRU–NATO)

The Euro-Atlantic Disaster Response Coordination Centre (EADRCC) is the focal point for coordinating disaster relief efforts of the 46 Euro-Atlantic Partnership Council (EAPC) nations in cases of natural, technological disasters and terrorist attacks within the EAPC geographical area. Its Weapons of Mass Destruction Disaster Management Centre has experts on CBRN.

- EADRCC informs the Secretary General of NATO and EAPC about any disasters and requests for international assistance, and coordinates the response within the EAPC area upon a request from a stricken country.

- EADRU comprises a non-standing, multinational mix of national civil and military elements (qualified personnel of rescue, medical and other units, equipment and materials, assets and transport), which remain under their respective national control operating under the 'EAPC flag' while deployed in the stricken country as an asset of the local emergency management authority.

- The local emergency management authority would be in overall control of operations in stricken areas, although the EADRCC would assist in coordinating the activities of the various national elements.

- EADRU acts in cooperation with the UN and other international organizations in disaster response. The UN Office for the Coordination of Humanitarian Affairs (OCHA) permanently bases a liaison office in the EADRCC in Brussels. The 'Oslo Guidelines' prepared by OCHA contain general principles for the utilization of military and civil defence assets in disaster relief situations.

- The UN Disaster Assessment and Coordination (UNDAC) Team is deployed to assess both the disaster situation in, and the requirements of, the stricken nation, or in its absence EADRU will organize another assessment team.

Web: www.nato.int/eadrcc

NATO Response Force

NATO Response Force can be deployed to operate in high-intensity environments and is able to draw on designated specialist capabilities. It has a civil emergency planning action plan and a multi-faceted military concept of operations for defence against terrorism.

- NATO's Chemical, Biological, Radiological and Defence Battalion will consist of teams from 13 nations. Possible scenarios include the threat or real use of weapons of mass destruction against military or civil objectives, industry, large-scale accidents, and outflows of dangerous materials caused by natural catastrophes.

- NATO is developing five CBRN capabilities: near real-time biodisease surveillance; expertise in the CBRN field; mobile laboratory; virtual stockpile – centre of expertise on CBRN; and decontamination of personnel and equipment.

Web: www.nato.org

UN Security Council (UNSC), Weapons of Mass Destruction Branch Department for Disarmament Affairs

The use or threat of chemical or biological weapons by one state against another will constitute a threat to international peace and security, and will fall within the response of the UNSC, to which the facts should promptly be reported. The Council:

- investigates in response to reports on the use of chemical and biological weapons in violation of the 1925 Geneva Protocol

- provides substantive support for the activities of the UN in the area of chemical, biological and nuclear weapons of mass destruction, including use of weapons of mass destruction in terrorist acts, as well as missiles

- cooperates with relevant intergovernmental organizations and specialized agencies of the UN system, in particular the International Atomic Energy Agency (IAEA), Organisation for the Prohibition of Chemical Weapons (OPCW), the Preparatory Commission for the Comprehensive Nuclear-Test Ban Treaty Organization, and the UN established Conventions on Terrorism.

Web: www.un.org

UN Office for the Coordination of Humanitarian Affairs (OCHA), UN Environment Programme (UNEP)

OCHA-Geneva has established an emergency response system for coordinating actions taken by the international community to deal with environmental emergencies and technological accidents. It is responsible for mobilizing and coordinating international disaster response, and can be contacted on a 24–hour basis in case of an emergency.

- The Organisation for the Prohibition of Chemical Weapons (OPCW) acts in cooperation with the OCHA Environmental Emergencies Section, which provides rapid coordination and mobilization of emergency response resources from the international donor community when requested by developing countries facing environmental emergencies.

- UNEP's involvement in environmental incidents includes chemical and oil spills, industrial accidents and other sudden crises with the potential for significant damage to the environment and human health and welfare.

- The Information Clearing House serves as a focal point to ensure available information on chemicals, maps and satellite images from donor sources and institutions is channelled directly to the relevant authority in the affected country.

Web: http://ochaonline.un.org and www.unep.org

International Programme on Chemical Safety (IPCS)

The INCHEM database of IPCS is a joint venture of the UN Environment Programme (UNEP), International Labour Organization (ILO) and the World Health Organization (WHO), established to carry out and disseminate evaluations of the effects of chemicals on human health and the environment. IPCS produces guidelines and training materials on preparedness for, and response to, chemical incidents that also involve deliberate release of chemical agents.

- More than 100 experts from all WHO regions contribute to WHO's chemical and biological scientific advisory group.

- IPCS provides information on chemicals, diagnosis and treatment and supports poison information centres in developing countries.

- The INTOX programme, which includes an electronically linked network of about 120 centres in 70 countries, allows rapid access to toxicological, analytical and clinical expertise. Such a mechanism could be useful in the identification of and response to incidents involving chemical agents used in warfare.

The INCHEM database is accessible free of charge.

Web: www.inchem.org and www.who.int/pcs

Inter-organisation Programme for the Sound Management of Chemicals (IOMC)

IOMC was established in 1995 by participating organizations: UN Environment Programme (UNEP), International Labour Organization (ILO), UN Food and Agriculture Organization (FAO), World Health Organization (WHO), UN Industrial Development Organization (UNIDO), Organisation for Economic Co-operation and Development (OECD), and UN Institute for Training and Research (UNITAR).

The purpose of IOMC is to promote coordination of the policies and activities pursued by participating organizations, jointly or separately, to achieve management of chemicals in relation to human health and the environment.

Web: www.unep.org

OECD/UNEP International Directory of Emergency Response Centres for Chemical Accidents

A joint publication of three organizations: Organisation for Economic Co-operation and Development (OECD), UN Environment Programme, Division of Technology, Industry, and Economics (UNEP-DTIE), and the Joint UNEP/OCHA (Office for the Coordination of Humanitarian Affairs) Environment Unit.

Provides information on centres for chemical incidents in 30 OECD and non-OECD countries. OECD Centres are national, regional or local, and provide emergency response services for chemical accidents under the responsibility of governments, industry or international organizations. They maintain a list of experts and/or information on preparedness for, or response to, land-based chemical accidents, or could quickly refer requests for information. Accessible to callers worldwide, 24 hours a day.

Web: www.oecd.org

Agency for Toxic Substances and Disease Registry (ATSDR)

ATSDR is an agency of the US Department of Health and Human Services, which performs specific functions concerning the effect on public health of hazardous substances in the environment.

ATSDR Emergency Response Teams are available 24 hours a day, and are comprised of toxicologists, physicians and other scientists available to assist in an emergency involving hazardous substances in the environment.

24–hour emergency number for health-related support in hazardous materials emergencies, including on-site assistance:

Tel: 24/7 emergency: (+1) 404 639 6360; Tel: (USA) 404 498 0110; Tel: (toll-free) 888 422 8737; Fax: 404 4980057

Web: www.atsdr.cdc.gov; E-mail: ATSDRIC@cdc.gov

National poisons centres

At country level, contact points include national poisons centres. A worldwide list of centres (YellowTox) is available at www.intox.org Contact details for local poisons centres can generally be found in telephone directories.

Health Protection Agency (HPA), UK National Poisons Information Service

■ Provides a year-round, 24–hour service for medical professionals and others to advise on the diagnosis, treatment and management of patients who may have been poisoned by chemicals. It provides information on chemical identification, chemical properties, toxic by-products, first aid measures, acute management, risk assessment and laboratory analysis.

■ It can also advise UK-based NGOs working overseas on suspicion of chemical releases and protective measures, such as decontamination and evacuation, toxicological advice on likely health effects, and clinical advice on antidotes and medical treatment.

Tel: +44 (0)870 600 6266 (accessible to UK-based international aid organizations working in middle- or low-income countries); Tel: +44 (0)20 7639 8999 (24–hour information and advice); Fax: +44 (0)20 771 5309

Web: www.hpa.org.uk (Organisations Divisions → and Units → Chemical Hazards and Poisons → National Poisons → Information Service)

Didcot (Headquarters), Cardiff, London, Newcastle, Birmingham.

Weather Check
For readings on weather conditions and wind direction in the event of a chemical attack in the UK and worldwide.

Tel: +44 (0)9001 333111

Conventions

1997 Convention on the Prohibition of the Development, Production and Stockpiling and Use of Chemical Weapons and Destruction (Chemical Weapons Convention, CWC)
The CWC is the first disarmament agreement negotiated within a multilateral framework that provides for the elimination of an entire category of weapons of mass destruction under universally applied international control.

- The Convention prohibits the development, production, acquisition, stockpiling, retention, transfer and use of chemical weapons. It also forbids state parties to assist, encourage or induce anyone to be involved in outlawed activities.

- The CWC stipulates that state parties must totally destroy their existing stockpiles of chemical weapons and the related production facilities located on their territory or under their jurisdiction or control within 10–15 years after the CWC's entry into force.

- The CWC established an international organization (Organisation for the Prohibition of Chemical Weapons, OPCW) to oversee its operation to ensure compliance to eliminate chemical weapons, verify destruction and monitor non-diversion of dual-use chemicals, and to facilitate mutual assistance and protection to all member states if threatened or attacked.

Web: www.opcw.org

1925 Geneva Protocol
Prohibits 'the use in war of asphyxiating, poisonous, or other gases and all analogous liquids, materials or devices' and also 'extends this prohibition to the use of bacteriological methods of warfare'. The prohibitions set out in the Protocol are now considered to have entered customary international law and are therefore binding even on states that are not parties to it.

Web: www.icrc.org/Web/Eng/siteeng0.nsf/html/genevaconventions

Biological epidemic alert and response mechanisms

World Health Organization (WHO)

WHO programmes provide technical assistance on various aspects of public health, including chemical and radiological accidents, surveillance of communicable diseases, global outbreak alert and response, chemical safety and mental health.

Development of new tools, within WHO's mandate, includes modelling of possible scenarios of natural occurrence, accidental release or deliberate use of biological and chemical agents and radionuclear material that affect health.

Web: www.who.int

Global Outbreak Alert and Response Network (GOARN)

WHO mobilizes international assistance through the GOARN, which provides up-to-date technical guidance on threats of biological and chemical agents. It provides a near real-time mechanism for systematically gathering infectious disease intelligence, detecting, rapidly identifiying and verifying epidemic emergencies of international concern. GOARN interlinks 110 existing networks which together possess the data, expertise and skills to keep the international community alert to outbreaks and ready to respond. It focuses technical and operational resources from scientific institutions, medical and surveillance initiatives, regional technical networks of laboratories, the UN Children's Fund (UNICEF), the Office of the UN High Commissioner for Refugees (UNHCR), Red Cross and Red Crescent Societies, and international humanitarian NGOs (International Rescue Committee, Médecins sans Frontières, Merlin and Epicentre).

- The WHO Communicable Disease Surveillance and Control Unit supports 31 national plans for surveillance and early warning, and strengthens national public health response and preparedness. It provides assistance to the national health ministry to train emergency mobile teams in management of complex emergency situations, controlling outbreak of disease, and conducting rapid health assessments.

- WHO's national pharmacist helps manage the essential and emergency drugs department.

- WHO provides vaccines and personnel for communicable disease response to the national health ministry.

- The Response Network is designed to send a mobile field unit anywhere in the world within 24 hours after an infectious disease outbreak is reported.

Web: www.who.int/csr (Disease Outbreak News)

Global Public Health Intelligence Network (GPHIN)

GPHIN is a semi-automated electronic system for real-time gathering of disease intelligence. It heightens vigilance by continuously and systematically trawling electronic data sources, identifying warning information, assessing and verifying alerts about epidemic threats and rumours of unusual disease outbreaks on a daily basis.

Web: www.who.int/csr/alertresponse/epidemicintelligence/en/

Early Warning and Response Network (EWARN)

EWARN was set up by WHO in partnership with NGOs present in the field. It is a community-based epidemic surveillance system that links 100 community organizations. The Pan America Health Organization is collaborating with WHO.

Web: www.who.int

WHO Integrated Capacity Development Programme for Laboratory Specialists

In order to strengthen national diagnostic and surveillance capacity at all levels, the Integrated Capacity Development Programme for Laboratory Specialists aims to:

- improve diagnostic capacity for infectious diseases and appropriate public health practices

- extend the network of national and international laboratories to ensure timely exchange of information

- ensure the availability of rapid, effective and secure means of transportation for diagnostic materials and laboratory samples.

Web: www.who.int/esr/en/

WHO Health Map

The Public Health Mapping Group provides:

- Geographic Information Systems for the convergence of disease-specific information and their analyses in relation to population settlements, surrounding social and health services and the natural environment.

- A database that produces maps at village, district, country and sub-regional levels. They can help planning of disease control activities or improve surveillance and health information systems.

Web: www.who.int/csr/mapping/en/index.html; E-mail: health_mapping@who.int

Centers for Disease Control and Prevention (CDC), USA

CDC's support activities include surveillance, clinical, epidemiological, environmental, laboratory work, communications, medical management and administration of prophylaxis, monitoring of adverse events and decontamination.

Web: www.cdc.gov

Biological Conventions

The 1975 Convention on the Prohibition of the Development, Production and Stockpiling of Bacteriological (Biological) and Toxin Weapons and on their Destruction (Biological Weapons Convention, BWC)

The operation of the BWC is reviewed at intervals of five or six years. The absence of any formal verification regime to monitor compliance has limited the effectiveness of the Convention.

Web: www.brad.ac.uk

Radiation information sources

Radiation Emergency Medical Preparedness and Response (WHO-REMPAN)

The WHO is a full party to the Convention on Early Notification of a Nuclear Accident and Assistance in the case of a radiological emergency or nuclear accident, for which the International Atomic Energy Agency (IAEA) is the focal point.

At WHO, radiation protection issues are addressed by the Radiation and Environmental Health Unit within the Department of Protection of the Human Environment, and in the Cluster on Sustainable Development and Healthy Environments.

WHO has established a network of coordinating centres, REMPAN, for radiation emergency preparedness and practical assistance and advice to victims in the case of overexposure from any source of radiation. REMPAN assistance in radiation emergencies includes:

- human resources specialists in medicine, health physics and radiology, as well as skilled nurses and technicians
- equipment to provide special medical assistance to overexposed persons, and portable equipment for radiation monitoring
- medical services for the diagnosis, prognosis, medical treatment and follow-up of persons affected by radiation
- scientific services with expertise to assess radiation doses and exposure
- transportation advice for affected persons
- specialized teams on a multinational basis to render medical assistance on site.

Web: www.who.int

Inter-Agency Committee on Response to Nuclear Accidents (IACRNA)

IACRNA provides a framework for cooperation of international organizations and the European Commission in the field of radiological emergency preparedness, to coordinate information response to radiological accidents.

Web: www.europa.eu.int

European Community Urgent Radiological Information Exchange System (ECURIE)

ECURIE is operational within the Environment Directorate on a 24/7 basis, and uses coded information to avoid language barriers. In the case of a nuclear accident, the main role of the EC is to receive an initial notification, to verify the message content, to launch the alert to all member states and the International Atomic Energy Agency (IAEA), and to receive and forward additional information to all member states.

Web: www.europa.eu.int

National bodies

Most countries should have a special body responsible for protection from and regulation of radiation exposure.

Ministry of the Russian Federation for Civil Defence, Emergency Situations and Migration of the Consequences of Natural Disasters (EMERCOM)

International cooperation agreements exist between the Government of Russia, Ministry of Foreign Affairs (EMERCOM) and UN OCHA. Activities of the National Disaster Management System of Russia include:

- civil defence, preparedness, search-and-rescue service, emergency prevention and response for radiation accidents and disasters, man-made disasters: chemical, biological and radiological.

- crisis management center, regional disaster management centres, disaster medical center, expeditionary airmobile hospital and regional emergency response units: stockpile of resources

- the Special Risk Operations Center has a Radiation, Chemical and Biological Reconnaissance and Monitoring Unit to identify contaminated areas and conduct urgent emergency response operations

- specialized distributive database on radioactive and chemical contamination of the environment, food and drinking water and radiation exposure of the population

- social protection of emergency-affected population and humanitarian activities in the event of chemical hazards and radiation emergencies; establishment of a new state system of emergency education and training of the population and industries.

Nuclear protection

International Atomic Energy Agency (IAEA), Vienna, Austria

Under the Convention for the Early Notification of a Nuclear Incident, the IAEA is the designated international organization officially notified by the affected country.

Its Safeguards Programme supervises nuclear reactors around the world to ensure radioactive material has not been diverted to a weapons programme, or notification may come via another member state to the EC Rapid Notification Procedures.

The IAEA emergency team has stockpiles including detection equipment.

Web: www.iaea.org

Conventions

Convention on Early Notification of a Nuclear Accident and Assistance

This Convention provides the prime legal instruments that establish an international framework to facilitate exchange of information and prompt provision of assistance in the event of radiation accidents, with the aim of minimizing the health consequences.

1996 Comprehensive Nuclear Test-Ban Treaty

The Treaty bans all nuclear explosions, for military or civil purposes.

1980 Convention on the Physical Protection of Nuclear Material

This Convention deals with the transport of plutonium and enriched uranium.

1970 Treaty on the Non-Proliferation of Nuclear Weapons and Additional Protocol

The Non-Proliferation Treaty is a landmark multilateral treaty to prevent the spread of nuclear weapons and weapons technology, and to further the goal of achieving nuclear disarmament.

188 states have joined the Treaty, including the five nuclear-weapons states.

Provisions of the Non-Proliferation Treaty include assistance to countries without nuclear plants to acquire technology for peaceful use, in return for refraining from the pursuit of nuclear weapons.

Explosive incidents

International Code of Conduct against Ballistic Missile Proliferation

There is no universally accepted norm of instrument specifically governing the development, testing, production, acquisition, transfer, deployment or use of missiles. The Code constitutes a voluntary, non-legally binding instrument.

International disaster/Crisis/Emergency response relief organizations and bodies

Office for the Coordination of Humanitarian Affairs (UN OCHA) – Civil Support to Crisis Response Organisations

Provides humanitarian support coordination and protection of civilian populations (situations of war, disaster, and weapons of mass destruction deployment).

Its civil emergency action planning with partner nations provides:

- an inventory of national capabilities

- minimum standards/guidelines to enhance interoperability between partners

- civil–military cooperation

- a register of medical experts and medical treatment of casualties.

Web: www.ocha.org

UN Disaster Assessment Coordination (UNDAC)

UNDAC teams can provide assessments of humanitarian needs in technical emergencies, in consultation with the government of the affected country. If international assistance is required on receipt of a warning of an imminent chemical threat to the civilian population, the UN Resident Coordinator and/or the UN Disaster Management Team would:

- contact the OCHA to exchange information on the disaster or threat; determine whether specialist assistance is required to plan and implement precautionary measures; ensure the necessary UN communication and information systems are ready and operational; and alert all relevant agencies for standby

- first priority would be to establish the need for immediate emergency measures to save and sustain the lives of survivors; second priority would be recovery and determining the type of assistance required

- UNDAC resources include a wide range of equipment and supplies: food, shelter, water capabilities, transportation assets, medical care, expert teams and disaster response contacts.

Web: www.ocha.org

UN OCHA Joint Logistics Coordination (UNJLC)

The UNJLC's mission is to complement and coordinate the logistics capabilities of cooperating humanitarian agencies during large-scale emergencies.

The UNJLC is activated through an inter-agency consultation among decision makers designated by the IASC-WG (Inter-Agency Standing Committee – Working Group). A decision is made within 24 hours on the basis of the scale of the crisis, existing agency capabilities, the extent of bottlenecks, possible use of military/civil defence assets, and situation assessments by the UNJLC unit.

Once the decision to activate is taken, the UNJLC will initiate deployment within 48 hours. To facilitate a swift deployment, various standby capacities are drawn on, including a special Flyaway Kit containing essential equipment, and information and communications technology support.

Web: www.reliefweb.int

UN OCHA Military Civil Defence Unit (MCDU)

OCHA's Military and Civil Defence Unit is the focal point in the UN humanitarian system for the mobilization and coordination of military and civil defence assistance where these are needed in response to humanitarian emergencies.

MCDU's Logistic Support Unit, which is responsible for the management of OCHA's stockpile of emergency relief items stored at the UN Humanitarian Response Depot in Brindisi, Italy, contains items such as tents, blankets, water supply and purification equipment, and electricity-generating equipment.

MCDU will only be considered when civilian capacities have been, or will become, overstretched. In the case of a major disaster, the coordination capacity of the stricken nation may need to be reinformed by either the utilization of a UN On-Site Operations Coordination Centre or deployment of an additional headquarters staff national element.

Web: www.reliefweb.int

UNDP Bureau for Crisis Prevention and Recovery (BCPR)

The BCPR assists country offices of the UNDP to provide a rapid and effective response to key challenges facing countries in crisis and post-conflict situations. These initiatives include small arms reduction, disarmament and demobilization, mine action, conflict prevention, peace-building and recovery.

Web: www.undp.org

World Food Programme (WFP)

In the event of long-term impacts on food security, WFP could incorporate activities to address the needs of victims of biological and chemical weapons in its recovery and development programmes. When potential threats to food security arise from the use of biological or chemical weapons, these could be factored into ongoing early warning and contingency planning exercises.

Web: www.wfp.org

European Union – Global Health Security Initiative

The Global Health Security Initiative was launched by health ministries of the G7 Group. The WHO participates as scientific consultant organization, and the Initiative collaborates with the Global Outbreak Alert and Response Network (GOARN), in strengthening epidemiology and laboratory capacity, and the International Programme on Chemical Safety (IPCS). The Initiative has:

- a communicable disease network, including a rapid alert system for any outbreak of infectious diseases, which focuses on coordination of public health emergency planning and preparedness, and the availability of treatments

- ability to draw on all member states' expertise (epidemiologists, microbiologists, logisticians) to assess what measures are needed for reinforcing warning systems, rapid response capacities, analytic capacity and surveillance

- a civil emergency planning action plan, with the future appointment of an European Coordinator for Civil Protection within the Commission

- extended cooperation to include pooling of expertise in the nuclear, biological and chemical fields, available 24 hours a day to assist any country that requests help

- enhanced cooperation on information-sharing concerning antidotes, vaccines, antibiotics and access to hospital treatment for any victims of such attacks

- a system of immediate, systematic exchange of information relating to incidents or threats of terrorist attack, and creation of a Civil Protection Monitoring and Information Centre in the Commission.

Web: www.pei.de/bioweapons/ghsi; www.eu.org; http://europa.eu.int

Council of Europe

The Council of Europe established the Multilateral Group on International Action against Terrorism. The Governmental Committee of Experts on Terrorism, set up by the Committee of Ministers in 2001, is responsible for coordinating and following up the counter-terrorist activities of the Council of Europe in the legal field. Published Guidelines on Human Rights and the Fight against Terrorism.

Web: www.europa.eu.int

European Union Action Programme – Community Mechanism for Civil Protection

This is an EU-wide capability for the timely detection and identification of biological and chemical agents that may be used in attacks, and for the rapid and reliable determination and diagnosis of relevant cases. Functions include:

- a response centre for all types of emergencies, CBRN, natural, environmental or technological (24/7), and to facilitate transport of resources

- an inventory of means of CBRN risk response in member states; availability of expertise as well as intervention teams

- a stock and health services database, and a stand-by facility for making medicines and healthcare specialists available in cases of suspected or unfolding attacks

- a 24/7 operational network to secure exchange of information, consultation and coordination on health matters potentially involving chemical and biological agents; also provides regular information exchange with the most relevant international organizations, mainly UN and NATO

- established the European Atomic Energy Community with mutual aid between states in the event of a radiological emergency

- facilitating and supporting actions undertaken by the Community or Member States, including identification of intervention teams, and establishment and dispatch of specialized personnel and expert assessment and coordination teams (within 12 hours) following a request for assistance

- assistance interventions, either conducted autonomously or as a contribution to an operation led by an international organization

- interface with the civil protection mechanism, the network for epidemiological surveillance and control of communicable disease – mutual consultation mechanism to deal with any crisis involving bioterrorist threat

- cooperation between different existing monitoring systems:

  BICHAT – rapid alert system of the health sector to allow prompt transmission of alerts and exchange of information between monitoring systems and the Commission in cooperation with International Atomic Energy Agency (IAEA), World Health Organization (WHO), World Meteorological Organization (WMO), NATO and Organisation for Economic Co-operation and Development (OECD).

- European Community Urgent Radiological Information Exchange (ECURIE)

- Common Emergency Communication and Information System(CECIS)

- a major project of general interest for all member states, involving processes of enhancing civil protection capabilities for dealing with disasters in certain significant aspects, such as prevention, preparedness, response, immediate aftercare, detection, and analysis of risk and vulnerability.

Web: www.europa.eu.int

European Community Joint Research Centre

Offers scientific and technical expertise in the nuclear, chemical and biological fields, and operates in networks with national laboratories and research centres on behalf of the Euratom Safeguards Office and the International Atomic Energy Agency (IAEA).

Operates the European Non-Proliferation Information and Analysis Centre.

Web: www.europa.eu.int

Global Health Security Action Group

Set up to implement the Global Health Plan. Activities include:

- action relating to the purchase and storage of medicines, and smallpox vaccines

- programme for interlinking P4 laboratories (equipped to study the most dangerous viruses)

- under the European Enter-net Programme, all member states, the World Health Organization (WHO), Pan American Health Organization (PAHO) and the European Commission are interconnected and can swiftly exchange data from national surveillance systems and information on particular types of suspect cases

- works with WHO on activities concerning bioterrorism, improving operational aspects of the Global Outbreak Alert and Response Network (GOARN) and its integrated approach to strengthening epidemiological and laboratory capacity

- strengthening the scientific basis required for CBRN surveillance activities.

Web: www.who.int

Global Security Newswire

Via the website of the Nuclear Threat Initiative, the National Journal Group provides a daily synopsis of nuclear, biological and chemical weapons and related issues from global news sources.

Web: www.nti.org

International Committee of Military Medicine

Cooperation exists between the International Committee of Military Medicine and the World Health Organization (WHO) to foster international civil–military cooperation in responding to disasters, including physical, radiological, chemical and biological hazards of natural origin.

NATO military medical assistance will be considered only if national relief organizations are inadequate, insufficient or non-existent. Military medical assistance will be provided at no cost to receiving states. Costs may be recoverable from the international organizations seeking assistance.

The website, which has restricted access, enables exchange of information and rules on health intervention plans, monitoring of diseases, contamination of water and food chains, and guidelines on accidental or deliberate origin.

Conventions

European Convention on the Recognition of the Legal Personality of International Non-Governmental Organizations

At present this is the only international standard-setting instrument on NGOs.

Quick reference cards

Card 1 Chemical agent indicators

■ Dead or dying people and animals

■ Unexplained casualties

■ Multiple casualties choking, fitting, disorientated, experiencing breathing difficulties

■ Observe any mist, spray, or low lying cloud of fog that is not related to the current weather conditions or has no logical explanation (such as proximity to a chemical plant site, tanker crash)

■ Any unusual odour

Card 2 Chemical attack

■ If an attack occurs while you are outdoors, take shelter quickly in the nearest building, close all windows/doors, and shut off the flow of air

■ Move upstairs, find an interior room, and seal the room

■ Remain inside until told it is safe to leave, then ventilate and vacate the shelter immediately

■ If an attack occurs indoors, open windows and breathe fresh air

■ Otherwise evacuate by stairs to street (using an escape hood if available)

■ Once protected from chemical agent exposure, decontaminate skin and hair by showering

Card 3 Biological agent indicators

- Sick or dying people, animals, fish or insects
- Unusual illness for the geographical region or time of year, such as large number of flu-like symptoms in summer season
- Unexplained/unconnected casualties from different areas presenting the same symptoms
- Clues that indicate a cluster of unusual illness may have a deliberate cause
- Large number of people with similar unexplained or unusual disease or syndrome or death
- Higher morbidity or mortality than expected with a common disease or syndrome
- Failure of a common disease to respond to usual therapy
- Endemic disease with unexplained increase in incidence
- Illness in people exposed to common ventilation systems
- Deaths or illness among animals that precede or accompany deaths or illness in humans
- Disease normally transmitted by a vector that is not present in the local area
- Unusual, atypical, genetically engineered or antiquated strain of agent
- A single case of disease caused by an uncommon agent (smallpox, some viral haemorrhagic fevers)
- A disease that is unusual for an age group
- A similar genetic type among agents isolated from distinct sources at different times or locations

Card 4 Radiological/nuclear exposure

Indicators

- Nausea, vomiting, diarrhoea (within one hour of radiological release)
- Fatigue, black 'burn' marks on skin

Actions

- Move out of the path of radioactive fallout cloud
- Take shelter as far underground as possible, or on upper floors of building
- Close windows and doors and shut down ventilation systems
- Find ways to cover skin, nose and mouth
- Decontaminate by removing clothing, and showering
- Consider food and water restrictions
- Consider evacuation or relocation

Card 5 Suspicious devices and explosives

- Do not use a radio or cell phone in close proximity to suspicious devices (within 500 feet, approximately 150 metres)
- If you find a suspect device with any of the following attached to it, treat as a chemical or biological improvised explosive device:
  - package containing compressed air cylinder with tubing or liquid container
  - unexplained munitions-like material (bomb)
  - radioactive dispersal device, ball bearings or metal fillings
  - nozzle or spraying device
  - material that seems to emit heat without any sign of an external heating source
  - containers that display a radiation symbol

Card 6 Individual action

- In a CBRNE incident, immediately put on your personal protective equipment (PPE)
- Remember the distance–time–shielding rule for protection
- Decontaminate as soon as possible
- Remain calm
- **Do not** go to the aid of casualties in the hazard (hot) zone without PPE

Card 7 Evacuation procedure

- Evacuate to a safer distance from the source of CBRNE exposure
- If leaving in a vehicle:
  - close all windows
  - turn off air-conditioning and close all air vents
  - assess the wind direction (flag on car)
  - immediately drive (5 km) upwind and re-assess the situation
  - send a radio warning to base
  - do not stop for any reason
  - do not re-enter the hot zone until it is safe to do so

Card 8 Sheltering in-place

Shelter in-place if a rapid or safe evacuation is not possible (no vehicle; hostilities)

- Get into the nearest building
- Move upwards to an interior room (toilet/bathroom) on a higher floor
- Close all windows, doors and air conditioning
- Put a wet towel across the bottom of the door
- Seal the doorframe and windows with duct tape
- Send a radio warning or report to base
- Accept the fact that you cannot help victims
- Do not attempt to move unless at greater risk; wait for rescue
- Carry out emergency decontamination procedure

Sheltering equipment and supplies

- Satellite phone and radio
- Flashlight with batteries
- First aid kit and scissors
- Replacement clothing
- Bedding
- Toiletries (including soap, sponge); household bleach
- Bottled drinking water
- Non-perishable foods (canned, dried or packaged food products)
- Heavy-duty rubbish bags with sealing supplies

Card 9 Emergency decontamination of people and equipment

- Take care no contact is made with any contaminant
- External surfaces of personal protective equipment (PPE) are likely to be contaminated
- Remove equipment outdoors, downwind of unprotected persons; the person who helps (still PPE-protected) touches only the external parts of the equipment
- If there is suspected toxic liquid on the equipment, wash first with soapy water
- Put disposable items in a plastic rubbish bag
- Decontaminate other equipment in soapy water solution, and rinse
- Discarded equipment should be buried (one metre deep)
- Decontaminate the whole body using 'rinse–wipe–rinse' method with soapy water

Card 10 The 1–2–3 Scene Safety Rule for emergency services

(1) One casualty: approach the scene using normal procedures

(2) Two casualties: approach with caution, report to emergency services

(3) Three casualties: do not go to the scene, stay at a safe distance (400 metres, 1300 feet)

Card 11 CHALETS casualty assessment

- Casualties – number of dead, injured and uninjured
- Hazards – present and potential
- Access and exit – best access routes for emergency vehicles
- Location – exact location of incident
- Emergency services – present and required
- Type of incident – brief details
- Safety – ensure the safety of everyone in the vicinity

Card 12 Incident report information

- Date, time, place, location of emergency
- Event history of incident – witness statement or observation
- Type of release – chemical, biological, radioactive, explosive
- Wind direction and speed – light breeze, strong winds, gale
- Plume information – size of cloud/vapour/direction of drift
- Magnitude – size of affected area and population
- Reported deaths and injuries
- Extent of damage to health facilities or services
- Expected health problems – priorities
- Has a state of emergency been declared?
- Other international or UN organizations present?
- What action is to be taken?
- Human resources required (number, type of personnel)

Glossary

Absorbent A tissue structure that is able to take in, or suck up and incorporate; involved in absorption

Acute exposure A single exposure to a substance or multiple exposures occurring within a short time, usually 24 hours or less

Aerosol Fine liquid or solid particles suspended in a gas, e.g. fog or smoke

Anthrax An infectious, usually fatal disease of warm-blooded animals, especially cattle and sheep, caused by the *Bacillus anthracis* bacterium. The bacterium exists as (dormant) spores which can live in soil; the spores are very resistant in the environment and may survive for decades in certain soil conditions

Antibiotic A substance that inhibits the growth of or kills microorganisms

Antitoxin An antibody formed in response to, and capable of neutralizing, a biological poison

Asphyxiants Substances that replace oxygen, eventually make breathing impossible

Atropine A compound used as an antidote for nerve agents

Bacteria Single-celled organisms that multiply by cell division and can cause disease in humans

Biochemicals Chemicals that make up, or are produced by, living things

Biological threats/agents Living organisms, or the material derived from them, that cause disease in, or harm to, humans, animals or plants, or cause deterioration of material

Biowarfare/biological warfare The intentional use of biological agents as weapons to kill or injure humans, animals or plants, or to damage equipment

Blister agent A chemical agent, also called a vesicant, which causes severe blistering and burns to tissues, skin, eyes and respiratory tract. Exposure is through liquid or vapour contact

Blood agent A chemical agent that interferes with the ability of blood to transport oxygen and causes asphyxiation. Examples include cyanogen and phosgene

Botulinum toxin One of the most poisonous bacterial substances known. The bacterium grows on poorly preserved food and causes a severe form of food poisoning

Brucellosis A bacterial infection that causes abortion in animals and is remittent in humans

Catastrophic or major incident Any emergency that requires mobilization of emergency services, national health services and local authorities for initial rescue and treatment of a large number of casualties and assistance to displaced people

Causative agent The organism or chemical responsible for causing a specific disease or harmful effects

Chemical incident An event in which there is, or could be, exposure of the public to chemical substances (toxic gas, liquid or solid) which cause, or have the potential to cause, ill health

Chemical warfare agent A chemical substance intended for use in military operations to kill, seriously injure or incapacitate people through its physiological effects

Chemical weapon Any munitions or devices specifically designed to inflict harm or cause death through the release of toxic chemicals

Cholinesterase An enzyme that regulates nerve impulses by breaking down acetylcholine to stop its action. Cholinesterase inhibition is associated with a variety of acute symptoms such as nausea, vomiting, blurred vision, stomach cramps and rapid heart rate

Choking agent Substance that causes physical injury to the lungs. Exposure is through inhalation. In extreme cases membranes swell and lungs become filled with liquid. Death results from lack of oxygen, hence, the victim is 'choked'

Chronic exposure Repeated exposure over a relatively long period

Cold zone The area beyond the inner cordon containing the hazard

Consequence management Measures to protect public health and safety, restore essential services, and provide emergency relief to business and individuals affected by the consequences of a crisis

Contagious Capable of being transmitted from one person to another

Contaminated casualty Any person who has come into contact with the contaminant and is physically injured or ill

Crisis management Measures to identify, acquire and plan the use of resources needed to anticipate, prevent and/or resolve a crisis or an act of terrorism

Culture A population of microorganisms grown in a medium

Cutaneous Relating to the skin

Decontamination The process of making people, objects or areas safe by absorbing, destroying, neutralizing, making harmless or removing the hazardous material

Detection Locating a signal indicating the presence of a potential hazard (but not necessarily quantification of the hazard)

Dirty bomb Use of common explosives to spread radioactive materials over a targeted area

Disaster Serious disruption in the normal functioning of a society that causes widespread human, material and environmental losses which exceed the ability of the society to cope using its own resources

Dose The amount of radiation absorbed over a period of time

Erythema Redness of the skin due to capillary dilatation

Etiological agents Living microorganisms or toxins that cause human disease

First responders Response persons or services applicable to a suspected chemical, biological or radiological incident

Fissile material An isotope that readily fissions after absorbing a neutron of energy

Fission The splitting of the nucleus of a heavy atom into two lighter nuclei. It is accompanied by the release of neutrons, X-rays, gamma rays, and the kinetic energy of the fission products

Gamma ray radiation High-energy electromagnetic radiation emitted by nuclei during nuclear reaction or radioactive decay. These rays have high energy and short wave length, and are potentially lethal to humans

Haemorrhagic fevers Any of the diverse group of diseases characterized by a sudden onset of symptoms including fever, aching, internal bleeding and shock. Includes Ebola, Lassa and Marburg

Hazards Natural or human-made elements that have the potential to materialize into harmful events

HazMat An accidental release of a substance, agent or material which results in illness or injury

Hot zone The zone of highest contamination. Only personnel in appropriate personal protective equipment (PPE) should enter this zone following risk assessment

Identification Determining the hazard by group and type

Immunization Artificially stimulating the body to develop antibodies against infectious disease by the administration of vaccines or antitoxins

Infectious agents Biological agents capable of multiplying in an infected host

Ingestion The act of swallowing

Inhalation The act of breathing in (can apply to radiation, biological or chemical toxic fumes)

Inhibitor Any substance that interferes with a chemical reaction, growth or other biological activity

Inner cordon Surrounds the immediate scene and provides security for it. Made up of hot and warm zones. Personnel within the inner cordon must wear appropriate personal protective equipment (PPE) commensurate to the risk

Inoculation Introduction into the body of the causative organism of a disease

Integrated emergency management A process for the development of flexible plans to enable any organization to deal effectively with any emergency, foreseen or unforeseen

Irritant or irritating agent An agent (chemical, biological or radiation) causing irritation

Lacrimation The act of secreting and discharging tears

Lifelines Essential resources critical to the survival of the community, including water, power, communications systems and transportation infrastructure

Liquid agent A chemical agent that presents as an oily film or droplets. The colour ranges from clear to brownish amber

Major incident The mobilization and organization of emergency services and supporting organizations in response to the threat of death, serious injury or displacement of a large number of people

Microorganism Any organism (e.g. bacteria and viruses) which can be seen only with a microscope

Monitoring A quantitative indication of the magnitude of a hazard over time

Nausea An unpleasant sensation usually preceding vomiting

Nerve agent A substance that interferes with the central nervous system

Non-persistent agent An agent that, on release, loses its ability to cause casualties after 10–15 minutes. Has a high evaporation rate; is considered a short-term hazard in ventilated areas

Nuclear blast An explosion with intense light, heat and a damaging pressure wave that spreads radioactive material that can contaminate air, water and ground surfaces for miles around

Odour Volatile emanation perceived by the sense of smell

Oedema Accumulation of an excessive amount of watery fluid in cells, tissues or cavities

Off-gassing The evaporation or release of a chemical substance

Organism Any individual living thing, whether animal or plant

Outer cordon Designates the controlled area into which unauthorized persons are not allowed entry

Pandemic A disease affecting or attacking the population of an extensive area (region, country or continent)

Parasite Any organism that lives in or on another organism without providing benefit

Pathogen Any living organism capable of producing serious disease or death

Persistent agent An agent that, on release, retains its ability to cause casualties for an extended period, usually from 30 minutes to several days. Usually has a low evaporation rate; its vapour is heavier than air. Considered to be a long-term hazard

Phosgene Carbonyl chlorine – a colourless liquid below 8.2°C, but an extremely poisonous gas at ordinary temperatures

Photophobia Abnormal visual intolerance to light

Plume Material spreading from a particle source and travelling through environmental media such as air or groundwater. Could describe the dispersal of particles, gases, vapours and aerosols in the atmosphere, or the movement of contamination through an aquifer

Q fever An infectious disease that is highly contagious, but rarely kills. It is transmitted from one person to another

Radiological dispersal device A device (weapon or equipment), other than a nuclear explosive device, designed to disperse material in order to cause destruction, damage or injury by means of the radiation produced by the decay of such material

Resuscitation The act of restoration to life. Re-establishment of heart and lung action after cardiac arrest or apparent sudden death

Ricin A poisonous protein extracted from the castor bean and used as a biochemical agent

Sarin A nerve poison which is a very potent, irreversible cholinesterase inhibitor; a more toxic nerve gas than tabun or soman

Smallpox An acute, highly contagious, sometimes fatal disease causing a high fever and widespread skin eruptions. Caused by a virus that may be airborne or spread by direct contact

Soman An extremely potent cholinesterase inhibitor

Spore A reproductive form some microorganisms take to become resistant to environmental conditions, such as extreme heat or cold, while in a resting stage

Surveillance The process of systematic collection, orderly consolidation and evaluation of persistent data with prompt dissemination of the results to those who need to know, particularly those in a position to act

Symptom Any perceptible change in the body or its functions that indicates disease

Toxic chemicals Any chemical that, through its chemical action on life processes, can cause death, temporary incapacitation or permanent harm to humans

Toxicity A measure of the harmful effects produced by a given amount of a toxin on a living organism

Toxins Substances, produced in some cases by disease-causing microorganisms, that are toxic to other living organisms. Toxins have a low volatility and are generally dispersed as aerosols. Primary hazard is inhalation

Tularaemia An infectious disease that chiefly affects rodents, but can also be transmitted to humans through insect bites or contact with infected animals. Certain strains can be deadly. Also called rabbit fever

Vaccine A preparation of killed or weakened microorganism products used to artificially induce immunity against a disease

Vapour agent A gaseous form of a chemical agent. If lighter than air, the cloud will rise and disperse more quickly

Vasoconstriction Decrease in the calibre of blood vessels

Vector An agent (e.g. an insect or rat) capable of transferring a pathogen from one organism to another

Venezuelan equine encephalitis (VEE) An airborne virus transmitted from animals to humans through mosquitoes that have fed on infected animals

Vesicant See *Blister agent*

Virus An infectious microorganism that exists as a particle rather than a complete cell

Volatility A measure of how readily a substance will vaporize

Vomiting agents Produce nausea and vomiting effects, can also cause coughing, sneezing, pain in nose and throat, nasal discharge

Vulnerability Can be divided into two components – susceptibility and resilience. Susceptibility is the determination of those hazards to which a community is exposed. Resilience is the ability to withstand the effects of those hazards

Weapon of mass destruction A chemical, biological or nuclear weapon

Endnotes

1. Additionally, an estimated 100 000 Iranian soldiers also survived Iraqi chemical attacks during the Iran–Iraq War. In 1990 the Iraqis were reported to have filled 100 R400 bombs and SCUD warheads with 10 000 litres botulinum toxin, 6500 litres anthrax and 1580 litres aflatoxin. These weapons were deployed in 1991 to four locations.

2. The protection offered by vaccine declines over a period which has not been precisely defined. Past experience during the era of natural smallpox infection suggested that protection lasted for up to six years. It may last longer if the person has been successfully vaccinated on multiple occasions. If health authorities determine that you have been exposed to smallpox or are at risk of infection, they would probably recommend that you be re-vaccinated immediately.

3. Vaccines currently available may not be protective when the exposure is unusual and characteristic of a biowarfare event (e.g. the anthrax vaccine may not protect against inhalation of weaponized spores).

4. Every major health authority recommends that administration of CBRNE antidotes or treatments should be performed only by competent medical personnel, citing significant risks from improper use and adverse reactions. No major health authority recommends stockpiling nerve agent antidote kits (auto-injectors) except at designated medical response facilities.

References

CIA (1998) *Chemical, Biological/Radiological Incident Handbook*. Washington, DC: Central Intelligence Agency.

Commission of European Communities (2002) *Civil Protection – Progress made in Implementing the Programme for Preparedness for Possible Emergencies*. Communication from the Commission to the Council and the European Parliament. Brussels: European Commission.

Department of Health, UK (2001) *Public Health Response to Deliberate Release of Biological and Chemical Agents*. London: Department of Health.

Dwyer, A., Eldridge, J. and Kernan, M. (2003) *Jane's Chem-Bio Handbook*, 2nd edn. Coulsdon, Surrey, UK: Jane's Information Group.

EMERCOM of Russia (1998) *Disasters and Man*. Monograph. The Russian Experience of Emergency Response. Moscow: EMERCOM of Russia.

GAO (2003) *Bioterrorism – Public Health Response to Anthrax Incidents of 2001*. Washington, DC: US General Accounting Office.

Gosden, C., Amitay, M., Gardener, D. and Amin, B. (1999) Open Forum: examining long-term severe health consequences of CBW use against civilian populations. *Disarmament Forum* 3, 67–71.

Henderson, D.A., O'Toole, T. and Inglesby, T.V. (eds) (2002) *Bioterrorism: Guidelines for Medical and Public Health Management*. Chicago, IL, USA: American Medical Association Press.

Heyer, R.J. (2001) *Introduction to NBC Terrorism*. Longmont, CO, USA: Disaster Preparedness and Emergency Response Association.

Hodgetts, T. and Mackway-Jones, K. (1995) *Major Incident Medical Management and Support: The Practical Approach*. London: BMJ Publishing Group.

Home Office (2003) *The Decontamination of People Exposed to Chemical, Biological, Radiological or Nuclear (CBRN) Substances or Material*. Strategic National Guidance. London: Home Office.

HPA (2003) *Medical Guide to Bio-terrorist or Related Threats*. Porton Down, UK: Health Protection Agency.

IAEA–WHO (2002) *Medical Preparedness and Response: Training for Radiation Emergency Preparedness & Response*. CD-ROM. Vienna: International Atomic Energy Agency.

IASC (2003) *Guidelines on the Use of Military and Civil Defence Assets to Support United Nations Humanitarian Activities in Complex Emergencies*. USA: Inter-Agency Standing Committee.

ICRC (2003a) *Explosive Remnants of War: The lethal legacy of modern armed conflict.* Geneva: International Committee of the Red Cross.

ICRC (2003b) *Report on Meeting of States on the Illicit Trade in Small Arms and Light Weapons.* Geneva: International Committee of the Red Cross.

IFRC/ICRC (1994) *The Code of Conduct for the International Federation of Red Cross and Red Crescent Movement and Non-Governmental Organizations in Disaster Relief.* Geneva: International Federation of Red Cross and Red Crescent Societies.

IMC/UCLA (2003) *Chemical, Biological and Radiological Threats, A Guide for Aid Workers,* CD-ROM. University of California, Los Angeles: International Medical Corps and Center for International Emergency Medicine.

Jane's (2003) *Mass Casualty Pre-hospital Handbook.* Coulsdon, Surrey, UK: Jane's Information Group.

de Jong, K. and Prosser, S. (2003) 'Weapons of mass destruction: chemical, biological warfare and mental health consequences.' Draft policy paper for Médecins sans Frontières–Holland.

Kelly, C. (2002) Humanitarian response to the use of weapons of mass destruction. *Humanitarian Times,* 20 November 2002.

Mashhadi, H. (2001) *Delivering Assistance and Protection.* OPCW Synthesis. The Hague: Organisation for the Prohibition of Chemical Weapons.

NATO (1996) *NATO Handbook on the Medical Aspects of NBC Defensive Operations.* Washington, D.C.: Departments of the Army, the Navy, and the Air Force, February 1996, (unclassified)

NATO (2001) *NATO Medical Handbook.* Brussels: Committee of the Medical Chiefs of Military Medical Services in NATO.

OECD (2004) *Recommendation of the Council Concerning Chemical Accident Prevention, Preparedness and Response.* Paris: Organisation for Economic Co-operation and Development. www.oecd.org/dataoecd/35/2/25990929.pdf

OPCW (2001) *Implementation of Article X of the Chemical Weapons Convention: Assistance and Protection against Chemical Weapons.* Note by the Secretariat. Unofficial electronic version (accessible via http://coe-dmha.org/CBRNE/linkedreferences/OPCW.doc). The Hague: Organisation for the Prohibition of Chemical Weapons.

Prehospital and Disaster Medicine 18 (1) 2003.

Prescott, G., Doull, L., Sondorp, E., Bower, H. and Aroop, M. (2002) *Hope for the Best, Prepare for the Worst: How humanitarian organisations can organise to respond to weapons of mass destruction.* London: School of Hygiene and Tropical Medicine/Merlin.

SCHR Position paper on *Humanitarian–Military Relations in the Provision of Humanitarian Assistance.* (accessible via www.itp.sssup.it/advancedreadings/humanitarian/steering_committee.pdf). Steering Committee for Humanitarian Response.

Sphere Project (2003) *Humanitarian Charter and Minimum Standards in Disaster Response.* Oxford, UK: Oxfam.

UN-OCHA (2003) *Guidelines on the use of military and civil defence assets to support UN humanitarian activities.* New York/Geneva: UN Office for the Coordination of Humanitarian Affairs. http://ochaonline.un.org

WHO (1999, 2003) *Rapid Health Assessment Protocols for Chemical Emergencies.* Geneva: World Health Organization.

references

WHO (2001) *Public Health Response to Biological and Chemical Weapons – WHO Guidance* 2nd Edition. Geneva: World Health Organization.

WHO (2002) *Preparedness for the Deliberate Use of Biological Agents: A Rational Approach to the Unthinkable.* Geneva: World Health Organization.

WHO (2003a) *Health Aspects of Biological, Chemical and Radionuclear Threats: Technical Guidelines.* CD-ROM. Geneva: World Health Organization.

WHO (2003b) *Communicable Disease Toolkit: Iraq Crisis, Guidelines for Outbreak Control.* Geneva: Communicable Diseases in Complex Emergencies Programme, Communicable Disease Cluster, World Health Organization.

WHO (2003c) Chemical emergencies. In: *Rapid Health Assessment Protocol for Emergencies.* Geneva: World Health Organization.

WHO-EMRO (2003) *Public Information on Biological and Chemical Threats.* Geneva: WHO Eastern Mediterranean Regional Office.

World Nuclear Association (2001)

Internet resources

Useful web addresses for CBRNE

The Brookings Institution
www.brook.edu

Center for Defense Information
www.cdi.org

Center for Nonproliferation Studies
www.cns.miis.edu

Chemical Safety Information from Intergovernmental Organizations (IPCS INCHEM)
www.inchem.org

Communicable Disease Surveillance Response
www.who.int
www.who.int/health_topics/infectious_diseases/en

Defence Science and Technology Laboratory
www.dstl.gov.uk

Emergency Preparedness and Response (CDC)
www.bt.cdc.gov

Federation of American Scientists, Chemical and Biological Weapons Control
www.fas.org

Foreign and Commonwealth Office (UK), Travel Advice
www.fco.gov.uk

International Atomic Energy Agency
www.iaea.org

Johns Hopkins University, Center for Civilian Biodefense Strategies, now affiliated with University of Pittsburg
www.hopkins-biodefense.org

Medical NBC Online Information Server
www.nbc-med.org

National Association of County and City Health Officials (NACCHO) –
Mobilization for Action through Planning and Partnership (MAPP)
http://mapp.naccho.org/MAPP_Home.asp

NetChemo.com – Nuclear, Biological, and Chemical Warfare Information
www.netchemo.com

Office for Domestic Preparedness, US Department of Homeland Security
www.ojp.usdoj.gov/odp/

Organisation for the Prohibition of Chemical Weapons
www.opcw.org

Public Health Laboratory Service, UK
www.phls.org.uk

RAND Corporation
www.rand.org

Saferworld (Nuclear Threat Initiative)
www.saferworld.org

UK Home Office
www.homeoffice.gov.uk

UK Resilience (UK Cabinet Office, Civil Contingencies Secretariat)
www.ukresilience.info

US Army Center for Health Promotion and Preventive Medicine
http://chppm-www.apgea.army.mil

US Army MEDCOM Quality Management Office – Nuclear Biological Chemical
Induced Illness
www.qmo.amedd.army.mil/chembio/chembio.htm

World Health Organization
www.who.org

Disaster and emergency management centres and networks

African Centre for Disaster Studies
http://acds.co.za

Asian Disaster Preparedness Centre, Bangkok
www.adpc.net/

Asian Disaster Reduction Center
www.adrc.or.jp

Biological and Toxin Weapons Convention
www.brad.ac.uk/acad

Bureau for Crisis Prevention and Recovery
www.undp.org

Canadian Centre for Emergency Preparedness
www.ccep.ca

CDC Emergency Preparedness and Response
www.bt.cdc.gov

Center for Defense Information
www.cdi.org

Center for Strategic and International Studies
www.csis.org

Center of Excellence in Disaster Management & Humanitarian Assistance
www.coe-dmha.org

Central Intelligence Agency, USA
www.cia.gov

Cranfield Disaster Management Centre
www.rmcs.cranfield.ac.uk

Department for International Development
www.dfid.gov.uk

Disaster Management Center, University of Wisconsin, USA
www.epdweb.engr.wisc.edu

Disaster Management Institute of South Africa
www.disaster.co.za

Disaster Research Center, University of Delaware, USA
www.udel.edu/DRC

eMedicine – Emergency Medicine
www.emedicine.com/emerg/index.shtml

Emergency Management Australia
www.ema.gov.au

Emergency Preparedness Information eXchange, Canada
http://epix.hazard.net

Federal Emergency Management Agency, US Department of Homeland Security
www.fema.gov

Food and Agriculture Organization of the UN
www.fao.org

internet

GlobalSecurity.org
www.globalsecurity.org

Nuclear Threat Initiative
www.nti.org

Pan-American Health Organization
www.paho.org

PubMed – National Library of Medicine
www.ncbi.nlm.nih.gov/PubMed/

Regional Disaster Information Center, Latin America and the Caribbean (CRID)
www.crid.desastres.net

St Louis University School of Public Health Center for the Study of Bioterrorism
http://bioterrorism.slu.edu

TOXBASE – National Poisons Information Service
(available to registered users, normally hospital departments or general
practitioners working in the UK National Health Service; not for public access)
www.spib.axl.co.uk

University of St Andrews – Bioterrorism Studies
www.st-andrews.ac.uk

US Army Medical Research Institute of Infectious Diseases
www.usamriid.army.mil

US Department of Health and Human Services
www.ndms.dhhs.gov

US Department of Justice
www.usdoj.gov

US Environmental Protection Agency, Emergency Prevention, Preparedness and
Response
www.epa.gov/swercepp

US Federal Bureau of Investigation
www.fbi.gov

Weapons of Mass Destruction – Civil Support Teams
www.defenselink.mil/specials/destruction

International organizations

British Red Cross Society
www.redcross.org.uk

Centre d'Etude des Risques Géologiques – Swiss Disaster Relief Unit
www.unige.ch/hazards

EC Humanitarian Aid Office (ECHO)
www.europa.eu.int/comm/echo/index_en.htm

Institute for Crisis, Disaster and Risk Management, George Washington University
www.gwu.edu/~icdrm/

InterAction – American Council for Voluntary International Action
www.interaction.org

International Committee of the Red Cross
www.icrc.org

International Council of Voluntary Agencies
www.icva.ch

International Federation of Red Cross and Red Crescent Societies
www.ifrc.org

International Institute for Environment and Development
www.iied.org

International Organization for Migration
www.iom.int

La Red (Disaster Prevention in Latin America)
www.desenredando.org

Médecins sans Frontières
www.msf.org

Merlin
www.merlin.org.uk

Office of the UN High Commissioner for Refugees (UNHCR)
www.unhcr.ch

Overseas Development Institute
www.odi.org.uk

Oxfam
www.oxfam.org.uk

RedR
www.redr.org

Reliefweb – Office for the Coordination of Humanitarian Affairs (OCHA)
www.reliefweb.int

SCF-UK Save the Children Fund
www.savethechildren.org.uk

UN Systems – Website Locator for United Nations System of Organizations
www.unsystem.org

internet

United Nations Development Programme (UNDP)
www.undp.org

US Agency for International Development (USAID)
www.usaid.gov

USAID Disaster Assistance
www.usaid.gov/our_work/humanitarian_assistance/disaster_assistance/

World Food Programme
www.wfp.org

World Health Organization
www.who.int

World Meteorological Organization
www.wmo.ch

Sources for PPE products

Aire Group
www.airegroup.com

BAE Systems
www.baesystems.com/newsroom

Centers for Disease Control and Prevention (US)
www.cdc.gov

Dräger Safety
www.draeger-safety.co.uk

Du Pont Personal Protection
www.tyvekprotech.com

Ferno Solutions
www.ferno.com

General Services Administration (US)
www.gsa.gov

Hughes
www.hughes-safety-showers.co.uk

Interspiro
www.interspiro.com

Protec Direct Ltd
www.protecdirect.co.uk

Respirex
www.respirex.co.uk

Scott Health & Safety
www.scottint.com

Siemens Environmental Systems
www.siemens.co.uk/env-sys/

Trelleborg Protective Products AB
www.trelleborg.com/protective

Mass decontamination tents and showers

Aireshower mobile decon unit
www.airegroup.com

British Fire Services standard decontamination unit
www.hughes-safety-showers.co.uk

MW Power Systems Ltd
www.mwpower.co.uk

Plysu
www.plysu.com

Index

index

Index

Index